From Zero to Hero

Write Your Short Film in 30 Days

FilmCraft

Published by Film Daily Media, LLC 2018
© 2018 Film Daily Media, LLC

All rights reserved. This book or any portion thereof may not be reproduced or used in any manner whatsoever without the express written permission of the publisher except for the use of brief quotations in a book review or scholarly journal.

First printing: 2018
ISBN 978-1-718-06341-9

Editor
Daisy Franklin
Editrix-in-Chief at *Film Daily, Bingewatch* & *FilmCraft*

Subeditor
Terence Whitley

Written by
Amy Roberts, Daisy Franklin, Luke Delaney

Research
Luke Delaney

Cover & chapter design
Taime Newton

great writers are indecent people
they live unfairly
saving the best part for paper.
– Charles Bukowski

Always now, forever independent

Film Daily is a platform connecting audiences with indie filmmakers via news, views, and reviews.

Our aim is to herald the golden age of the auteur and give everyone the tools to become a creator.

We keep you entertained about entertainment.

We believe film and TV are great catalysts for change and aim to empower our audience to use these media to bring about change in the global community.

We're your guide to:

Outsider storytelling emphasizing equality and diversity

Film education & the craft of filmmaking & screenwriting

The industry, film festivals, and film platforms

Current film news

Breaking into the business of content creation

Join our community at **https://filmdaily.co**

Table of Contents

Welcome, welcome — 1

How to use this book — 7

Day 1. People of letters: Screenwriting through the ages — 10

Day 2. Lights, camera, action: A brief but badass history of film — 14

Day 3. Short films: The short cut to a career in film — 20

Day 4. Late nights, inky fingers, RSI: Why do you want to be a screenwriter, anyway? — 26

Day 5. Make research your BFF, pt. 1 — 32

Day 6. Phantom Thread: Finding your muse — 38

Day 7. Avoiding the slush pile: Why your great idea might not actually be filmable — 44

Day 8. Make research your BFF, pt. 2 — 48

Day 9. WTF is genre, anyway? — 52

Day 10. Augment your craft with the best tech tools — 56

Day 11. What's a logline got to do with it? ... 60

Day 12. Find your voice – and stick with it. ... 64

Day 13. The hero's journey in 5 minutes ... 68

Day 14. Beginning, middle, and end . . . not always in that order ... 74

Day 15. Plot like Dr. Evil: Get on track & stay on it. ... 82

Day 16. Dialogue that kills ... 86

Day 17. Monologues: To be, or not to be? ... 92

Day 18. "Earl Grey, hot": Craft characters you can believe in. ... 96

Day 19. Tears for days: How to make the audience care ... 102

Day 20. The bigger the baddie, the bolder the victory ... 106

Day 21. Enter late – get out early. ... 110

Day 22. Bourne again: Infuse your characters with purpose & motivation. ... 114

Day 23. It Follows: How to write seamless scenes ... 118

Day 24. Who likes short shorts? — 124

Day 25. Be a writer – not a director. — 128

Day 26. Polished perfection: How your script should look — 130

Day 27. The cutting room: Handling rewrites — 138

Day 28. Beg, steal, or borrow a proofreader. — 142

Day 29. Pride comes before a fall: Every writer needs readers. — 146

Day 30. Make the fat lady sing: Give birth to your script baby. — 150

Day 31. Manage – don't micromanage – your creative team. — 154

Epilogue — 159

Bibliography

Welcome, welcome

Congratulations – you did it! The very virtue of picking up this book sets your intention to become a screenwriter.

However: buyer beware! A writing career in the entertainment industry is not all gold typewriters and namechecks in Johnny Depp acceptance speeches. To get from zero to hero in this game is a long, blister-inducing road.

Ready to dive in?

Always now, forever independent

There are a ton of screenwriting books out there, and I'm stoked you picked ours. This book was written in 2018 for thoroughly modern filmmakers. Stories have been told since the dawn of time, and we've expanded on the wisdom of our elders to create a bite-sized screenwriting guide made for our fast-paced society.

You're not a guinea pig; every method, technique, and mistake has been tried and tested (sometimes many times over) by our dedicated team of award-winning indie filmmakers and screenwriters. We've consulted experts, pored over books, and produced (terrible and hopefully not-so-terrible) content time and time again using these tips. We can't promise you a career in Hollywood, but we *do* promise to help you create a short film script which could assist you in breaking into the industry.

We're in a golden age for content production

As technology has connected the world, our ability to build community has grown. We're living in a golden age for content production. It's cheaper than ever to create content, and there are more opportunities than ever for your stories to be heard. "Development hell" is fast becoming a thing of the past. People have an insatiable appetite for content, and producers make serious moves every day to buy it.

The gates to Hollywood are being smashed down. Social media, streaming services, film festivals, and pitching events connect writers with development executives. Thanks to the internet, many voices and types of stories can find an audience. If you're a writer with a unique project, there's never been a better time to sell it than now.

In this multifaceted cultural climate, entertainment companies are always on the lookout for the new voices. To pursue a career in the media, you don't have to move to LA and wait tables looking for your big break. All you need is a computer, a reliable internet connection, and a passport.

Movies ain't the only game in town for someone with screenwriting skills

In our networked society, content really is king. It's everywhere you look. People are telling stories all the time, and you're probably exposed to hundreds everyday – from the video commercial showing at the local gas station to your morning news show, and from your favorite podcast to the ad you catch on your daily news website. People are telling stories and we're all listening (sometimes).

If you're listening to a story that's been produced, it's highly likely that story was created, or at least massaged, by a scriptwriter. Scriptwriters write advertising content, news scripts, explainer videos, award-winning podcasts, web videos, and jingles, as well as features, shorts, and TV shows. The skills you're about to learn *are* transferable – and there's a lot of work out there for folks with a poised pen and some hustle.

That being said, screenwriting is not necessarily an easy gig.

Ready to put in your 10,000 hours (writing)?

There is nothing to writing. All you do is sit down at a typewriter and bleed.
– Ernest Hemingway

A long time ago (in 1993) a dude called Malcolm Gladwell said nearly anyone can master any skill if they put in 10,000 hours of practice. While I think that sounds like a pretty arbitrary number (which scientists have gleefully been trying to debunk for the past 25 years), I do agree that practice makes perfect. If you're dreaming of a career as a screenwriter, first you gotta talk some truth to your good self.

Do you even like writing? You don't have to be an award-winning writer to become a screenwriter, but you do need some skills when it comes to the old clickety-clack (keyboard). If staring at a computer screen for hours at a time bleeding onto your script sounds like a bummer, maybe screenwriting isn't the job for you.

Many screenwriters enjoyed early careers as writers. Diablo Cody (*Juno*) was a blogger, Paul Schrader (*Taxi Driver*) was a film critic, and Jonathan Ames (*You Were Never Really Here*) was a novelist & columnist. Screenwriters live to tell stories. If storytelling isn't your thang, you might want to consider another gig in the biz.

Not got 10,000 hours under your belt, but still want to be a screenwriter? Better get writing now!

Ready to put in your 10,000 hours (watching)?

Part of being a great storyteller is conveying complicated notions in a way your viewers can understand. Writers are observers: they watch situations and attempt to comprehend why people act in a certain way. Great writers infuse their characters with humanity. Even when we don't agree with a character's actions, we must have an idea of the motivation behind them.

Writers find inspiration in the most banal situations: that mundane conversation with a bank teller, the Friday night catch-up with friends, or an apres-cinema teardown could all be inspiration for a future character.

Not all writerly inspiration has to come from real life – if ya wanna write the movies, ya gotta watch the movies. In the Year of our Lord Netflix 2018, it's tricky to keep a screening schedule, but try you must. As screenwriters, it's our job to understand trends, tropes, genres, and current content, and the best way to understand the climate is to watch, watch, then watch some more.

Once your ass is numb and inspiration strikes, you can thank us.

Ready to get rich quick? (Find another career.)

Humans are obsessed with redemption stories (see "Day 13: The Hero's Journey 5 Minutes"). We love to hear about businessmen who lost it all (Richard Branson, anyone?) and rebuilt their fortunes, as well as the overnight successes of people who were working as a waitress in a cocktail bar one minute and walking the red carpet at the Chinese Theatre the next.

The thing the papers always leave out of their neatly written career synopses is just how hard said waitress hustled to break out of that artisan eatery and break into Hollywood. As Eddie Cantor said, "It takes 20 years to make an overnight success."

In our networked society, the demands for fresh content are constant. Production companies can't keep up with the demand for fresh new content. Considering content is more economical than ever to produce (thanks to cheap hard- & software, geographic arbitrage via tax incentives, and other cost juggling) and new online production companies pop up regularly, betting on a new career, second career, or hobby as a content writer may not actually be a bad financial move. All the new opportunities mean it doesn't take as much time as it once did to find your footing (i.e., your first paid gig).

Ready to get RSI, back pain, and criticism? How about staring at a computer screen for many, many hours?

Let's get real for a second. Writing is a large part of being a screenwriter, and screenwriters are an essential cog in the content production machine. The only time you write on your own schedule is when you're working on a spec script (i.e., no $$$).

If you're getting paid to write, you have deadlines, colleagues, and a whole peanut gallery of people with opinions to please. You're under a lot of pressure to deliver, even on a low-budget indie piece. If you've been hired to write a script, say bye-bye to drinks after work and hello to hours hunched over a computer screen furiously typing to meet your deadline.

Working screenwriters don't have the luxury of writer's block. In a production team you need to write quickly and proficiently – *and* take feedback on board. In fact, being precious about your work is a surefire way to miss out on those next gigs.

We writers may be sensitive souls, but we have to develop a thick skin as soon as we get invited to a writers' room. Add to that our shortsightedness from staring at computer screens, rickets from never going outside, and chronic use injuries, and it's amazing we scrub up so well for photocalls at The Oscars.

So get out your reading glasses, stretch your thumb muscles, lay out your comfiest sweats-and-T-shirt combo, and get your favorite snacks ready. You're about to become a superhero: someone who can make people laugh with a word and cry with a camera direction.

If you're ready to embark on your new adventure as a writer, I'll shut up so you can get started.

– Daisy Franklin, Editrix-In-Chief
FilmCraft
June 2018

How to use this book

This book is your guide to writing a short film in thirty days. We're here to help you tie yourself to your computer and crank out a script in 30 days – *without* giving up your job, relationships, and social life (completely).

But there are many ways to feed a cat. Below is a quick guide to the many ways you can use this book.

The basic approach

Carve yourself between one and two hours (60 - 120 minutes) to dedicate to your script every day for thirty days. You don't have to chose consecutive days – you can take a break – but you do have to handle each lesson in order. After the 30th day, bask in the glory of being a newly minted screenwriter. Welcome to the club!

As a guide to sharpen an existing project

You might already have a script in the can (or nearly so) that needs a little more *oomph*. Or you think your script doesn't flow or has another flaw. With our thirty-day guide, you can workshop the steps to help you get your existing project ship-shape.

The binge

You've taken a week (or two weeks or a month) off to write your script – you're gonna do it no matter what! You're not afraid of trash talk from your family or bleeding fingers from marathon typing sessions. You binge this book a lesson at a time while applying it to your *Citizen Kane* in the making. After seven days (or 14, or 28) you relax, exhausted and with a shiny new script ready to be uploaded to The Black List.

The tortoise

Scriptwriting is on your list, but so is eating out, a vacation, a business venture, or an anniversary. You dive into the book when you have time, and after a while you've completed all the lessons and are ready to write your script. You use this book as a reference when typing up your script, and in a year or two you have a great script to make you proud.

The watcher

If you're more visually motivated, we got your back! We made a whole video education series to support this book. Because you're so special, you can get lifetime access to the video series for a mere $5 (from $30). You're welcome.

Email us to take advantage of this offer at **write@filmdaily.co**.

However you do it – do it well.

However you decide to use this book, make sure you do it right. We can't promise you an Academy Award, but we can promise if you follow our lessons, you'll be able to structure and tell your story in the most effective way possible. You'll be screenwriting like a boss very, very soon.

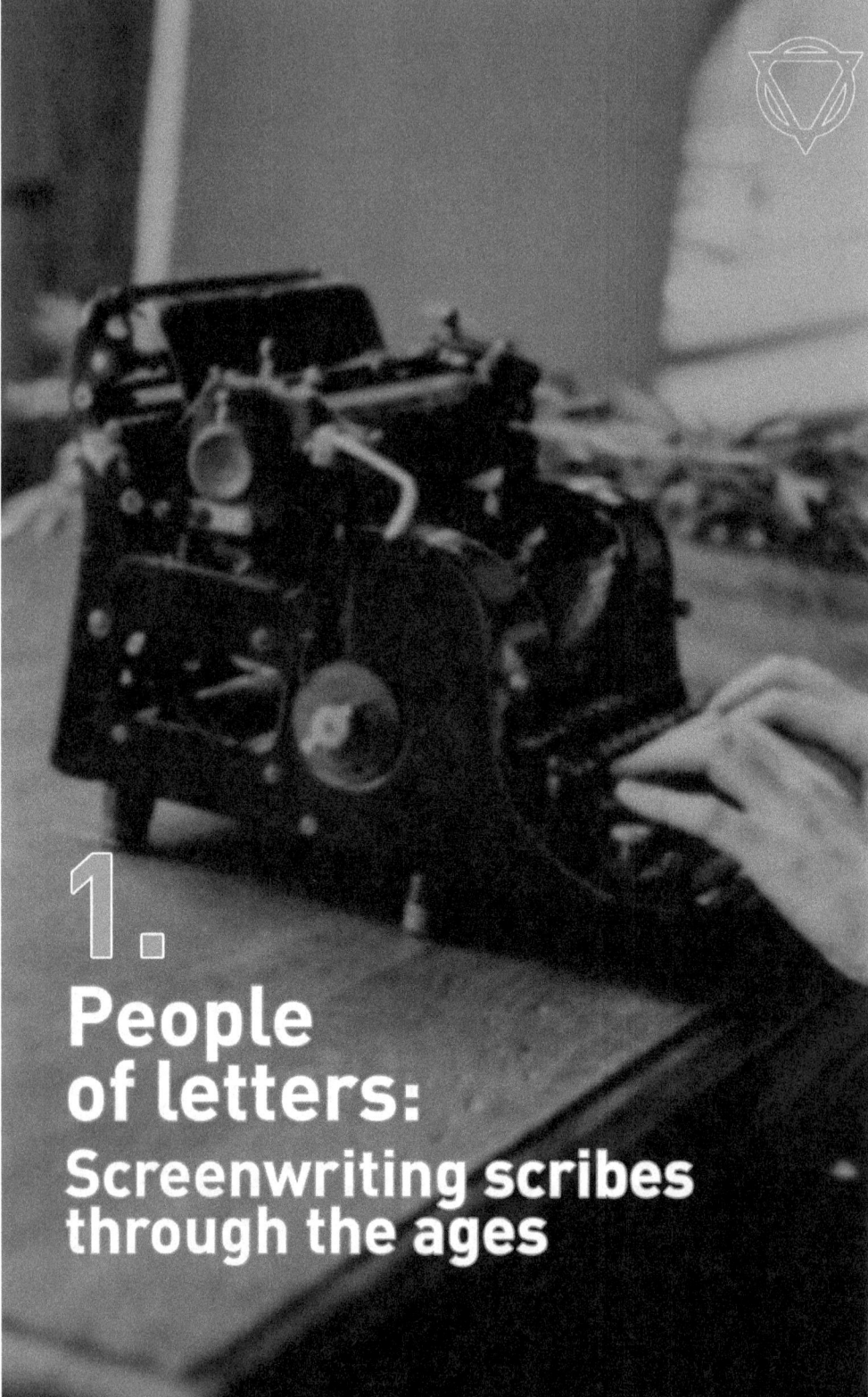

1.
People of letters:
Screenwriting scribes through the ages

Ready to bring the ruckus with the hottest movie script the world has ever seen? Just sit down and listen up. If you wanna be the future of screenwriting, you'll need to study the history of the artform first.

The earliest known screenplay was referred to as a "scenario", and later "continuity script". It broke down what actors did and added some camera angles.

In 1902, French director George Méliès was the first to break the mold with the screenplay for his revolutionary short film, *A Trip to the Moon*. With a bullet-point breakdown of everything Méliès wanted on screen, his continuity script was still succinct. One of the benefits of the silent movie era was its conspicuous lack of audio dialogue.

The "continuity script" then evolved into the elegantly named "master scene format", used by Edwin Porter in 1903 for his apparently epic 12-minute movie *The Great Train Robbery*. Bear in mind that twelve cinematic minutes in 1903 was the Zack Snyder superhero saga of today.

Scripts soon mutated into their final form: the *screenplay*. Over the years, the format of the screenplay has been adjusted slightly, even if the idea has remained the same. In the early days of the screenplay, for instance, people wasted perfectly good paper on elaborate notes about camera angles and editing. Maybe they even added some lunch orders, too. But as films grew longer, screenplays tightened up.

Nowadays, screenplays only include key information. What characters are in the scene? What the heck are they up to? Are they inside or outside? Is it day or is it night? What's their vibe, where are they, and what dialogue – if any – are they serving up? If you're a dude trying to flesh out a manic pixie dream girl fantasy, you might even want to include the clothes they're wearing or the sick tunes they're listening to – but we don't recommend it.

By all accounts, the screenplay as we know it is basic as all get-out; however, as proven by 90% of the tripe coming out of the Hollywood machine, it's still so easy to get wrong.

But don't worry – we got you. You're gonna be bringing that screenwriting ruckus in no time.

Homework

- What sort of school would we be if we didn't give you some tricky homework? Now make like a teacher's pet and rock your first homework assignment at screenwriting school.
- Watch *A Trip to the Moon* on YouTube.
- Grab your notebook and note down what you see on screen.
- You've just written the script for a visually oriented movie. Well done. (In your face, writer's block! Being a screenwriter is easy!!)
- Now that you have a little practice, try to find the script of your favorite film online.
- Make like you're watching Scandi Noir and read along with the movie. Make sure you have easy access to that pause button.
- Make a note of what changes you see. What changes were made between the script and the shoot?
- How have the actors infused their roles with humor, humanity, authenticity? Think about the other ways they could have played the characters (given the lines in the script).
- Observe how the screenwriter has been able to get across the visual narrative of the movie in the fewest words possible.
- Make a note of the way the director has interpreted the work of the screenwriter.
- Make a note of any times you feel the director has changed the setting or interpretation of the screenplay.

Now, think about the script you have just read. What is it about the title that makes it unique? What makes it stand out? Get out your notebook and start finding adjectives that best describe the vibe of your movie.

Resources

Log onto Film Daily and search our Craft articles for great scripts to download. Here are a few examples to get you started:

https://filmdaily.co/craft/read-the-scariest-screenplays-for-free/

https://filmdaily.co/obsessions/read-the-funniest-film-screenplays-free/

A Trip to The Moon
https://www.youtube.com/watch?v=BNLZntSdyKE

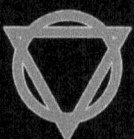

2.
Lights, camera, action:
A brief but badass history of film

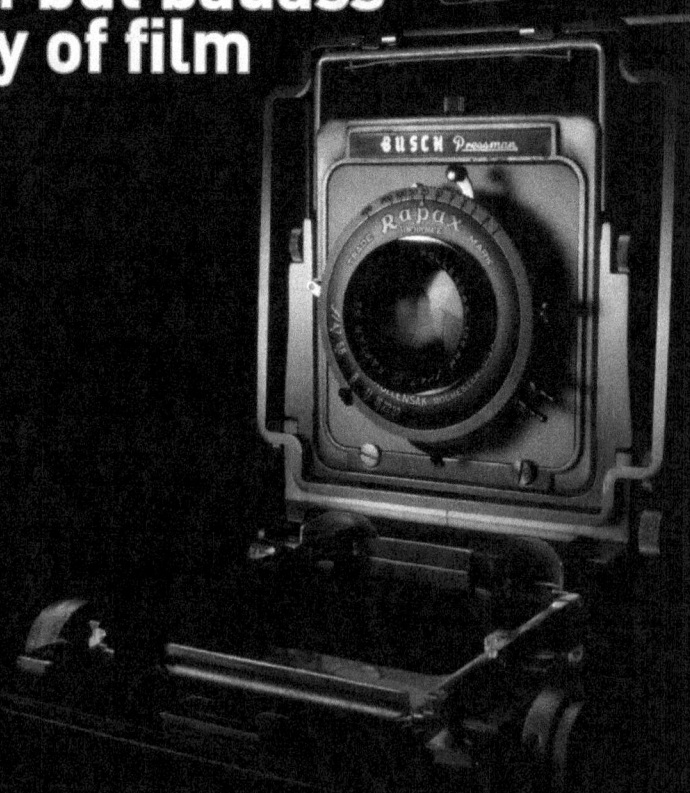

We get it. You're kind of a big deal just waiting to happen, with a winning screenplay screaming to be unleashed. But now you've blown through the history of screenwriting, it's probably also helpful to brush up on motion picture history too. So throw on something to make you feel intellectual and appreciate the finer details of how film first came to be.

By creating the phonograph in 1887, ya boy Thomas Edison essentially created the first moving image – a feat that various madcap inventors the world over were driving themselves crazy for years trying to figure out.

From there, the Lumière Brothers were moved to make their own movie, after seeing a demonstration of the phonograph-inspired kinetoscope in France. As you likely remember from various exciting museum trips as a kid, this early moving-image device allowed a single viewer to watch images in sequence through a peephole.

Infused with creative zeal, the Lumière Brothers went on to develop the first-ever film projector for their rookie cinematic effort, *Employees Leaving the Lumière Factory*. A stationary camera was left outside the building exits, where it captured the excitable bustle of that "Friday feeling" as dozens of workers hauled ass out of there.

The Brothers' idea was to capture movement to leverage the new technology to its utmost, which explains why we call them "the movies" rather than "the statics".

Arguably however, the main man of cinema was the ever inventive George Méliès. He lay the groundwork for modern filmmaking by writing scripts, building massive sets, and hiring huge casts and crews to bring his iconoclastic visions to life. The trailblazing filmmaker made over 400 films between 1899 and 1912, a figure sure to make every aspiring storyteller feel like a slacking underachiever. *Thanks a lot, George.*

Méliès also created some of the first-ever special effects, as witnessed in *A Trip to the Moon*. The pock-faced satellite is portrayed as a gurning peeping tom as space aliens get walloped into a dusty plume of smoke. He even developed the first color films by employing a cadre of twenty-one women to paint every single cell by hand. Glorious Technicolor was invented in 1916, around the same time the film audio track was introduced.

While many were delighted by this boom in technology, not everyone was eager to move with the times. Original hipster Charlie Chaplin preferred to keep it way old-school by holding off from using sound in his movies for decades. Chaplin went on to co-found his film production company United Artists, where he had complete control over his films, including the 1940 hit *The Great Dictator*. That particular flick proved Chaplin's formidable talents as a spoken actor, having delivered one of the greatest movie speeches of all time.

The 50s saw the French New Wave blow a plume of rebellious smoke in the face of Old Hollywood, before stubbing the butt into conventional storytelling. The cinematic movement introduced the idea that viewers didn't need to have their hands held though the journey of a story, letting them perceive moments in their own way.

Many of the films we know and love today were influenced by this new approach. Instead of offering a passive cinematic experience, French New Wave films catalyzed audiences to reflect on their own lives, experiences, and feelings.

Of course, the intervening decades have brought a few advancements in cinema. 3D movies popped the action out of the screen and into our faces; IMAX immersed us so deep we could feel it in our guts; Smell-o-vision lasted about a week in the 60s and made everyone feel kinda gross; and Michael Bay has continued randomly blowing things up. But no matter how cinema has evolved, it's always been about one core idea: great storytelling.

In our next lesson, we're gonna blow your mind by delving into how exceptional storytelling and big narratives can come in small presentations – and how tiny cinematic tales could be your first step to a colossal career.

Homework

By now, you're probably feeling like you've got this screenwriting thing all locked down, so you'll be ready for your next assignment. Grab a drink, make sure you've eaten, stick on your favorite tunes, and get ready for another A on your homework.

We're going to start easy again today with a little light watching.

- Watch a Charlie Chaplin silent movie – then watch another *with* recorded sound.
- Get out your notebook and list the differences between the two movies.
- Pull up *Film Daily* (and watch *Le Detour* by Michel Gondry, shot entirely on iPhone.
- Observe and listen to the way the short film uses sounds to tell the story. Perceive the clever and charming effects both visually and auditorily.
  After watching *Le Detour*, answer the following:

- Would the story be as powerful without the sound effects?
- What emotions are conveyed through sound, rather than images?
- How does the little red bike character emotionally grab the viewer?
- How do the sound effects add to the overall viewer experience?
- How does Gondry promote the idea of travel through this short?
- How is comedy expressed through sound?
- How does the film balance sound and visuals to create a compelling narrative?

Extra credit 1

If you want to get ahead by watching these other short films from a variety of genres:

- *Luna*: a compelling drama
- *Tick Tock*: a mind-bending story prompting multiple viewings
- *Lights Out*: 3 minutes of sheer terror
- *The Black Hole*: a simple and hilarious sci-fi comedy

Make notes about what makes these films stand out so much. What are the key plot points? How do they use sound to tell their stories?

Extra credit 2

Decide if you want to pen your movie under your own name or if you'd prefer to use a nom de plume. If it's the latter, start getting creative with the name you'd like to be known as. Need inspiration? Try this fake name generator tool - `https://www.fakenamegenerator.com/`

Resources

Luna
https://www.youtube.com/watch?v=5j-eYK4sTbg

Tick Tock
https://www.youtube.com/watch?v=w14v4vGUDdg

Lights Out
https://www.youtube.com/watch?v=kNbJE0y29_c

The Black Hole
https://www.youtube.com/watch?v=P5_Msrdg3Hk&t=9s

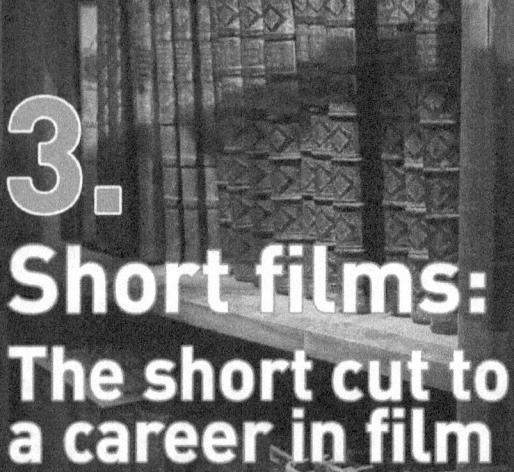

3.
Short films:
The short cut to a career in film

If you already have a big idea for your screenplay, you could be tempted to explore it as fully as possible with a rambling ninety-page script. No matter how tall your story is though, it could make a superior short film instead.

Back when film was scaring delicate everymen into thinking a train was about to plow into them, all films were short. Only when feature films became a thing did the term "short" get introduced.

Subsequently, short films were demoted to the opening act before a feature film: the cinematic equivalent of your friend's sister's boyfriend's band playing at 7:15 for the three of you and the bartender. The short film, or B-movie as it became known, remained in this position until being replaced by the far more lucrative visual assault of – you guessed it – advertisements.

As the birth of the B-movie proved, there was – and still is – a lot to be gained from the short film.

In the 30s, B-movies began as an affordable option during the Great Depression, as U.S. production companies scrimped for dollars to throw at entertainment. Though some B-movies lasted as long as 80 minutes, others would be shorter to open up for the headlining *A-movie*. When played on their own, B-movies would often be combined in thrilling double bills, giving horny teenagers across America a chance to get to first base.

B-movies were a big deal – Stanley Kubrick even made one, called *The Killing*. They provided a living for many and helped hundreds of independent cinemas gain footfall from cheaply made movies.

B-movies reigned for 40 years, but fell into redundancy when home television became popular, and horny teenagers discovered they could get way beyond first base in the comfort of their own couch.

The change was bittersweet. Many indie picturehouses went out of business, but in turn the short film became the medium of choice for wannabe filmmakers. Film festivals increased in number and became a breeding ground for exceptional filmmakers to showcase skills and vision – *without* significant budget. In fact, many of the greatest filmmakers of our time began their careers with short films.

George Lucas started with his short *THX 1138* before expanding it into a full feature. Ridley Scott proved his filmmaking prowess in 1965 with *Boy and Bicycle*; Martin Scorsese launched his colossal career with *The Big Shave* in 1967; Lynn Ramsay asserted herself as a tremendous talent with *Gasman* in 1997; and Damien

Chazelle initially made a short film called *Whiplash* in 2013, later expanding it into his Oscar-nominated feature of the same name.

Shorts have also helped launch momentous TV careers. *The Simpsons* originally began as a series of shorts for *The Tracey Ullman Show* in 1987, before becoming a primetime animated sitcom in 1989.

Ilana Glazer and Abbi Jacobson's *Broad City* began as a web series of shorts in 2009 before becoming a sitcom on Comedy Central in 2014. Likewise, Issa Rae's web series of shorts *Awkward Black Girl* helped pave the way for her HBO comedy series, *Insecure*.

Shorts are the novice filmmaker's calling card and a crucial tool to help you and your work get noticed. They demonstrate the genius you can wield on a coin purse of a budget and suggest the incredible feats possible, if someone would only throw fat bags of cash at you.

There's also plenty of encouragement from the industry for short film production. Both the Academy Awards and the BAFTAs have several award categories dedicated to the medium, providing prestigious accolades to animated and live-action shorts alike.

Dig deep into the vast world of independent film festivals, and you'll find most offer categories celebrating short film, while others are dedicated solely to the medium.

Such competitions seek out new talent by seeing who can achieve the most in a short time frame. If auteurs can make us laugh, cry, tremble in fear, or experience a life-altering epiphany in less than 15 minutes, what can they do with 80?

Short films offer a crucial playground for experimentation, because learning by doing is imperative for the aspiring filmmaker – especially when you encounter failure and find yourself staring into a movie misfire that also happens to have your name on it. This occurs to the best of us, but failure does offer an opportunity for growth.

Even the greatest filmmakers have likely experienced the same blows as you when starting out. You can invest huge time, effort, and creativity into a script, only to watch it implode into a trashcan fire of a film which in no way resembles your original vision.

But at least it was only a short film, the ideal starter for aspiring filmmakers. When one goes well, it can be your first small step to a big career; and when a short doesn't quite go as planned, at least it offers a chance to make affordable, constructive mistakes without putting you off writing or filmmaking forever.

All you need now is to look deep inside yourself and ask: why is it you want to become a screenwriter? Light some incense and prepare to get enlightened, because in our next lesson we're gonna bust this question wide open and explore the *whys* of screenwriting.

Homework

Task 1
Make it long or short

- Get out your handy notebook.
- Watch the feature film *Whiplash*.
- Then watch its short film predecessor.
- Make notes about how the short film was adapted to create a feature. Is there anything the feature lacked? Were the two films just as impactful as each other?

Task 2
Short film fests are the best

- Look online for a short film festival that takes place near you.
- Look through its website and social media platforms. Note down the type of movies it screens and make sure to watch any notable movies it premiered. Record the next event date and make damn sure you go!

Extra credit 1
Networking doesn't feel like working

Networking is like gold dust in this game. You never know whom you could meet out there. The more irons in your fire, the more opportunities come your way.

- Look online for some local writing communities. We suggest searching Meetup groups, local colleges, Eventbrite, Craigslist, and Facebook groups.
- Make a note of every online or IRL event you want to attend. Try and get to at least one event every few weeks.

Extra credit 2

- Think about the titles of the movies you find while interacting with your new filmmaker friends on social media, is there anything about them that inspires the name for your movie?

Resources

Whiplash short film
https://www.youtube.com/watch?v=lH8MOkk1OKs&t=163s

Whiplash DVD

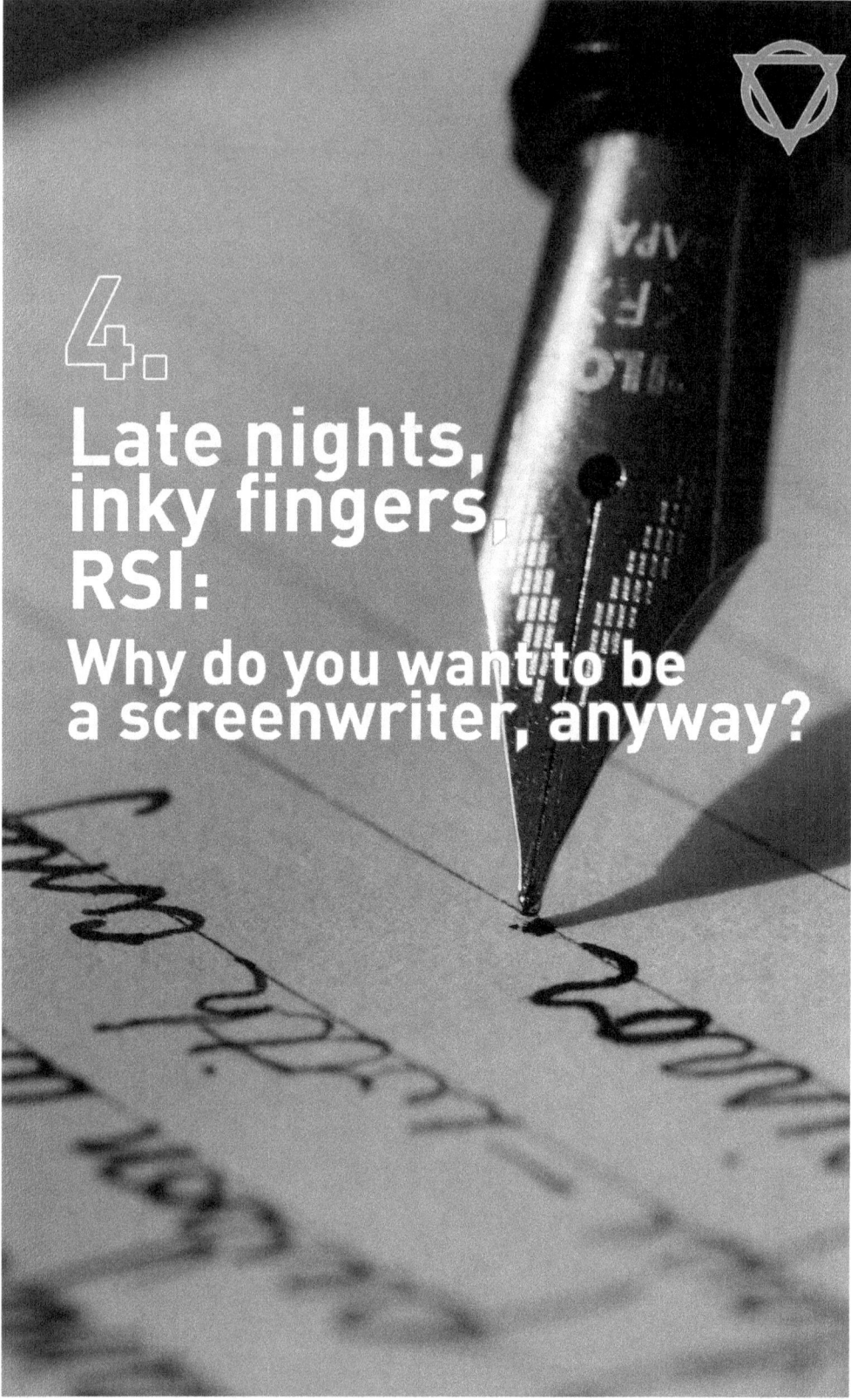

4.
Late nights, inky fingers, RSI:
Why do you want to be a screenwriter, anyway?

Are you sitting comfortably? We're about to dive into one of the most important questions about screenwriting: why do you want to do it? Hopefully your answer isn't "to get super-rich super quickly", because we don't have close to enough time to explain the problems with that.

We've got a hunch you want to write a screenplay because you've been influenced by other outstanding movies. Something about these films struck a chord and made you *feel*. Maybe they even reflected deep truths about who you are, your values, and your life experiences.

A great film can plunge a hand deep into your soul and pull out a fistful of emotions, leaving you curled up and weeping on your couch at two in the morning, covered in Dorito dust.

These stories resonate because they have something to *say*. They aren't simply a storytelling snack serving up empty cinematic calories. These are stories with substance, sending out a clear message.

In Disney Pixar's *Inside Out*, Joy adamantly believes happiness is the only emotion Riley needs. As the movie progresses, Joy learns sadness is just as necessary. Through various heartbreaking scenes that may or may not have made us weep in public, *Inside Out* explores a powerful notion: if we don't know how to channel sadness, we'll struggle to cope with everyday obstacles.

The lip-tremblingly poignant message of *Inside Out* is that it's okay to be sad. This is the secret behind Pixar's success: carrying strong yet universal emotional messages, their movies speak to *everyone*.

The same principle applies to television screenwriting. In HBO's *Game of Thrones*, Samwell Tarly learns he shouldn't waste his life just reading about the stories and the achievements of others. The series is a great example of an ongoing story with a variety of bold messages. The plot is entertaining, but also has the power to make you feel all sorts of crazy emotions about dragons, weddings, and an endlessly impending winter.

Most writers strive for this in their work: using the power of visual storytelling to get their piece of mind across. As story guru Christopher Vogler suggests, "Stories are metaphors and comparisons for how we feel about life."

What are you passionate about that needs to be shared with the world? What really riles you up? In this seemingly bottomless helter-skelter of life, what wisdom have you gained, and what statement do you want to make about it?

Keep asking yourself these questions. Delve deep. Got something? Good! Hold onto it; write it on your wall in big letters, bake a cake and ice it on the top … hire a skywriter and thread the words through the clouds, because congratulations! You've just found the theme for your screenplay.

This is the core message you want to get across with your story. If you don't have anything to say, chances are your screenplay won't get noticed. All great stories merit a great message.

However basic, even films like *Transformers* have a message. The theme of those blockbuster movies is often "Every sentient being has a right to freedom." It may be corny, but this gives the story a message of clear substance.

Likewise, in James Cameron's *Titanic*, the message is: we shouldn't seek meaningless material treasures, but rather something important, like true love – and sexy nude drawings. This message is boldly accentuated in the last act, when Rose casually throws the prized Heart of the Ocean diamond necklace off the side of the ship like a set of day-glo Mardi Gras beads.

When musing about what message you want your screenplay to convey, think of it as the giant magnet in the center of your story that pulls everything into place: every beat must point towards it.

If you're an amateur writer looking to create a big impact on a wide audience, it's crucial to spend time developing the theme of your screenplay. The more universal your message, the more individuals with whom your screenplay will strike a chord.

Now that you've taken a deep look inside yourself and found your story's theme, you want to give your screenplay microscopic detail and magnificent scope. Next lesson, we're going to the library to open a big old book called research.

Homework
Task 1
A long time ago in a galaxy far, far away

1. Get out yer handy notebook.
2. Watch the great sci-fi shorts which you can find in the resources section below.
3. Note down what you think the key point is that the writer wants to get across in each film.
4. Is this a universal theme – can everyone relate to the message?

5. Is this movie representative of its time period? Why do you think this movie was made at that time?
6. Think about your own movie. Why would someone want to see it? Why does your message relate to what's happening now?

Task 2

Bleed on paper: Get better at writing

- Search for dictionary, thesaurus, urban dictionary, grammar, and spelling apps.
- Download them onto your smartphone.
- Reconcile to check these apps anytime you find a word you don't understand.
- Add these words to your personal lexicon, whether compiled in a notebook, in your smartphone notes, on a Trello board, etc.

Task 3

Tap, tap, tap: Learn to type

Want to be a screenwriter, but can't type to save your life? Never fear – try these awesome typing games to get your fingers tip-tapping! It's gamified learning, fun and free.

```
https://sense-lang.org/typing/typing-race/?provider=senselang
```

Extra credit

Throw around some ideas for your movie names – write five potential names down and sleep on them.

– DAY 4

Resources

Nothing decent on TV tonight? Try a couple of these free, legal streaming websites to study films on:

```
https://tubitv.com/

https://www.snagfilms.com/

https://www.popcornflix.com/
```

Great sci-fi shorts

R'ha
```
https://www.rocketstock.com/blog/10-of-the-greatest-sci-fi-short-films-of-all-time/
```

Pets
```
https://www.youtube.com/watch?v=lBg67f3GzJM
```

Breaker
```
https://www.youtube.com/watch?v=R5kV6fyp7I4
```

5.
Make research your BFF, pt. 1

You've got the creative spark, the swagger of a genius, and the pearl of a story idea – but do you know the deepest, darkest secrets of your screenplay yet? All it takes is a little – or quite a lot of – research.

The most obvious type of screenplay requiring research is the biopic, an exploration into the life of an extraordinary individual. Unfortunately, you can't produce such a script by sitting back in your easy chair and imagining what Susan B. Anthony or Marcus Aurelius liked to do in their downtime.

In order to find out about people, experiences, events, communities, or even hypothetical sci-fi realms, you need to leap out of your comfort zone and step into that world. Use your phone for more than selfies with your cat and start calling significant people.

If you snag important interviews, shadow people in specific professions, and read anything and everything available on the subject of your screenplay, your writing will take its fullest form.

And if you're breaking out in a sweat at the thought of having to strike up conversation with a stranger, just chill. There are basic techniques you can use to overcome the debilitating shyness we like to call Writer's Shock.

It helps to know your interview subject might be just as shy as you, so take the time to make your interviewee at ease. Buy them a coffee or some lunch, break the ice with small talk, and if you suddenly feel cocky, crack a joke or three.

The more comfortable your interview subjects are, the more forthcoming they'll be. If you conduct an interview well enough, you might even learn obscure personal details few others know of. The aim of the conversation is to get to the *unseen*. You're Indiana Jones, and this is the mysterious artefact in the ancient cave.

In order to portray your subject respectfully, you'll need to understand it deeply. This is especially important when writing about a real-life person who has real-life feelings and real-life loved ones who wouldn't appreciate you flinging your real lively imagination onto their real-ass lives.

Some writers actually insist interviews are the most exciting part of writing. We're not sure we agree, but we can confirm the importance of diving deeply, even into minor details.

No need to write an encyclopedia entry – comprehensive notes, maybe even a dedicated folder of research, will suffice. Don't mire your masterpiece in endless detail.

Instead, collect your research with a strong sense of purpose. The story always comes first and *it* should guide you to the ideas requiring more realism.

You want fascinating details that make your screenplay pop off the screen. They should be essential and fitting, yet sparing and tasteful. Ask yourself: will this add to the authenticity of the scene – or am I bludgeoning my story with an Acme mallet of overkill? Finding the perfect balance between information and narrative will make your script shine.

Ready for the easy part? Research means you get to watch endless TV shows and movies. The point is to help you understand what's been done already, so you can take the same subject further by adding your singular spin.

Thorough research will place you among the greats. Truman Capote wrote *In Cold Blood* after traveling to Kansas to immerse himself in the community where four brutal killings took place. He even befriended the murderer to gather key insights into the mind of a potential killer, taking his dedication to storytelling to new (and terrifying) extremes.

Don't compromise your concept. Infuse it with prestige, respect, and detail. Research is key – but so is a solid idea.

Still need a little extra help finding those final nuggets of inspiration? Next lesson, we're going to help you find your muse.

Homework
Task 1
Get organized

It's time to get organized. We greatly prefer digital research tools rather than dusty paper, greasy pens, and index cards, but if that works for you, we hear ya. Here are our favorite online tools for organizing your research:

Evernote
evernote.com

If you've been living under a rock and haven't heard of Evernote, here's a quick debrief. The app is an online organization tool in which you can share your great ideas, favorite articles, documents, images, videos … you name it! Everything can be categorized to your liking and you can create collaborative boards with your friends they can add to on the go.

Trello
trello.com

Trello is the ultimate workflow organizer that works in the visual way we screenwriters think. Once you start with Trello, we warn you all other scheduling tools may look inferior. In fact, we just gave away a bunch of notebooks because Trello does that job so well.

This app allows you to organize your projects in workflow lists and drag cards through the various stages of your project. You can organize everything in your screenwriting process, from arranging interviews, to storing articles, to scheduling films and TV you need to watch.

Here's an example of a board you can use to help organize your process. Feel free to copy this board and use it to plan your screenplay.

`https://trello.com/b/aNoHyFBw/my-screenplay-research`

Are you just an old-fashioned guy/gal?

Like to keep things old school? Here are our tips for the traditional screenwriter.

- Go to the stationery store and buy yourself a nice folder with paper, file dividers, hole punches, highlighters, and those plastic folder thingies.
- Do web searches on every single thing you can find on your subject.
- If it has even the slightest impact on your understanding on the subject, go to the library and print that sucker! Get it in the folder. (Bonus points if you actually still own a printer.)
- Highlight the most important parts.
- Hey! While you're at the library, see what books you can find. Find anything pertinent in any of those books? Scan and print that MF.
- Send at least 5 emails to people you think could be of use to your story, and ask to interview them. Tempt them with coffee, or if they're busy, just make it a short phone call. (Make sure you specify it's for a film you're writing, or you'll just be a stranger asking them out on a date.)

- If it's appropriate, ask if you can record the interview – you're very interested in this person's opinion and don't want to forget anything.
- Taking physical notes is also fine. If you take notes, make sure you store them in the folder!

Task 2

Lists are friends

- Download the app List for Writers.
- Make some organization lists pertaining to your project.
- Use the app to add thoughts and ideas every time you get a new one. Eventually, you'll have a goldmine of information to build your characters from.

Extra credit

Come back to your movie titles. Do you still like them? Take a poll of your three favorite choices with your family & friends.

6.
Phantom Thread:
Finding your muse

Ever sat in front of a blank screen for a solid hour and not come up with a *single* bright idea? Sometimes your fountain of inspiration is reduced to a rusty set of pipes coughing up nothing but dust and social media procrastination.

Here's the thing about inspiration: it probably won't come if you're just sitting there willing it to happen – but it's essential to discover it.

In the Paul Thomas Anderson movie *Phantom Thread*, we see Daniel Day Lewis's revered dressmaker struggling to rediscover his genius. Without inspiration, he's nothing but a man holding limp scraps of fabric. He leaves the frustrations of his studio for dinner, where he unexpectedly meets his muse – and is transformed. He's dropping the most bomb gowns you've ever seen! He can barely keep up with his own genius!

Don't expect to make the killer garment of your screenplay just because you have the fabric. Find your muse and be active in your pursuit, and you'll find your work transformed.

Try taking the pressure off by reading a book – it's something you should be doing anyway as a writer. The act of delving into another world could be enough to ignite the creative firecracker you thought was a dud. Chances are the writer whose work you're reading did the same.

Go for a walk. Fill your vision with anything besides the four walls of your home, which can keep your creativity on lockdown.

If you want to take that walk to the next level, treat yourself to a coffee or a beer. A luxuriant afternoon in your favorite café or bar might awaken your dormant muse. Absorb the subtleties of human nature happening all around you.

Take notes of your observations: the conversation, the customers, the staff. Detail the personalities, presence, and habits of the people around you. Then *stop*.

Enjoy your drink, read a book, and bask in the simple pleasure of doing nothing. Don't even look at what you've written until the next day, then have another crack at creating a story using your notes. This doesn't work for everyone, but it might be just the technique you need.

Still drawing a blank? Watch a film – the finest homework there is a for a screenwriter, and a surefire way to find inspiration from a treasured writer or director.

Hunt for stories in newspapers. Even the tackiest tabloid dreck can be full of leads for your script. Look for the most eye-catching headlines: the ones that make you laugh, shudder with horror, or feel concern for the plight of humanity. They all could inspire a brilliant film idea.

Wrangle ideas out of the fortress of your imagination by blasting them out with music. This isn't just a fine excuse for you to spark up a phat one to your favorite jam; it's scientifically proven that music can relax and inspire you to work. Put together a playlist that emboldens your creative sensibilities: a soundtrack that molds your ideas into boisterous characters, dialogue, and setups.

Go old-school: leave your computer and put pen to paper for a while. Write it all down. Screenwriting guru Syd Field revealed that hesitating at every passing thought could trigger his writer's block. Original or not, write it anyway.

After all, writing garbage is an integral part of writing. Even Ernest Hemingway confessed he wrote one page of masterpiece to ninety-nine pages of crud, and so can you. If we didn't write garbage, we wouldn't know what was good! Embrace your inner trash heap.

Lastly, it might be worth trying a technique some writers swear by called "morning pages". Keep a notepad on your bedside table and start writing in it the second you wake up. This form of freewriting is just scribbling down whatever sleepy nonsense rattles around your brain while it struggles to figure out why in the hell you're awake and doing things at this ungodly hour.

In between descriptions of the questionable microwave burrito eaten at 2am and the weird dream about winning a drag race against Meryl "Speeding Wheels" Streep can lie the most wonderful and unexpected gems of inspiration.

So write it down. Five pages – no more, no less. Get used to writing when you don't want to, and discover the hidden depths of your imagination.

These exercises should result in one or more glorious ideas worthy of screenwriting pursuit. In our next lesson, we'll look at what makes an idea film-worthy, and ask whether yours can be translated to the big or small screen.

Homework
Task 1
If you want to be a writer, you need to be a reader

Not a big reader? If you want to be a writer, you need to become one. It doesn't really matter what type of book you read; we just need to get your creative juices flowing.

Task 2
Decompress from time to time

Do you ever feel claustrophobic living your day-to-day life? Are you a city-dweller, or just busy as hell? Make some time for *you* and you'll be a better writer. You can't sit in front of your computer all day, everyday.

Here are some tips to get out of your head and clear those cobwebs:

- Go for a walk in nature – enjoy your free time.
- Take a weekend vacation, or unplug all your devices and enjoy a weekend staycation at home.
- Start meditating.
- Pro tip: whenever you get stuck with your screenplay, just do a little exercise.

We recommend the following apps: Calm, Buddhify, Headspace, The Mindfulness App.

Task 3
Get out into the world

- Take yourself out for a coffee or drink.
- Open up your favorite news app – we like News 360 & Feedly.
- Read over the headlines of the day. For inspiration, save anything related to the subject of your screenplay.
- Revisit the headlines anytime you're stuck with your screenplay.
- Inspiration will soon strike!

Task 4
Listen up!

Still stuck? Listening to music is scientifically proven to make people more creative, so blast out some sick tunes to help you get your groove back.

Focus@Will is a music app that uses data science to provide you with inspirational music. There are various musical sounds to listen to while you work, each tailored to different types of brains. Dig in!

Task 5
First thing I do in the morning

Morning Pages are a stream-of-consciousness exercise you write first thing in the morning just as you wake up.

- Keep a notebook on your bedside table.
- First thing every morning for 5 days, write the first things that come into your head.
- Consult your Morning Pages any time you get stuck in your writing. Most could be garbage – but some can contain the gems of absolute genius.

Extra credit

Compare your working movie title with Paul Thomas Anderson's:

- *Hard Eight*
- *Boogie Nights*
- *Magnolia*
- *Punch-Drunk Love*
- *There Will Be Blood*
- *The Master*
- *Phantom Thread*

Is the name you've chosen as powerful? Why do you think his movie names work?

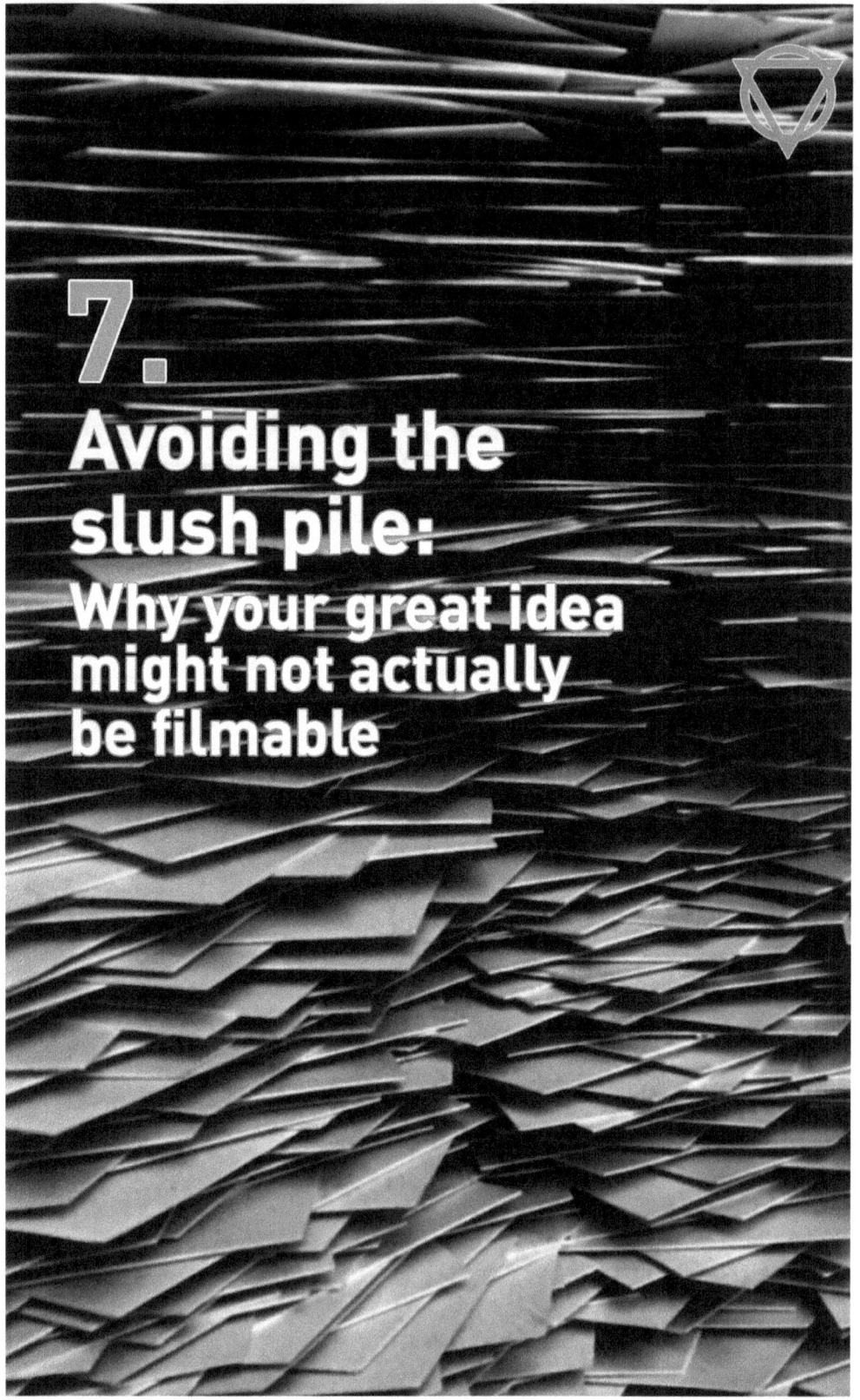

7.
Avoiding the slush pile:
Why your great idea might not actually be filmable

You've just sweated over a script with an ambitious setting. The opener? "EXT. EMPIRE STATE BUILDING – NEW YORK CITY – DAY".

A sweeping, panoramic shot runs across the epic Manhattan skyline. As we approach the Empire State Building, we see a toddler, a dog, and a sassy alien flying in from stage right. A giant octopus suddenly pulls itself out through one of the windows! The trio shoots lasers from their eyes as they speed toward it.

But be real: as epic, weird, and cinematic as it may be, is it filmable as a short?

Unless you have an uncle owed a debt by the Empire State Building or a cousin with a top-notch computer animation studio, this ambitious shot and location are tricky, to say the least.

The beauty of the short film is its potentially small budget. Opt for impressive stories instead of impressive set pieces and keep the logistics of your narrative down to the bare minimum. Every aspect – from the characters and locations to special effects – must be achievable.

We'd all love to have the freedom of storytelling without worrying about the dollars. But if your film isn't logistically possible with a threadbare budget, your cinematic dream might become a deluded fantasy.

It's possible to tell huge stories in small frames. Think of Joel Schumacher's *Phonebooth*, in which Colin Farrell spends 80 minutes freaking out within a single claustrophobic location – or Quentin Tarantino's *Reservoir Dogs*, set almost entirely in a small warehouse in Los Angeles.

These movies were producer favorites, because they came with the sweet guarantee of low production cost. Even Hollywood loves a bargain.

Here's an example of a simple short story idea, featuring a minimal cast and minimal locations, that would be a cinch to film:

A woman, afraid of the outside world, notices a man through her living room window – he's scorchingly hot. A total stud. Watching this man walk past her window at the same time every day becomes an obsession. She watches. She swoons. She falls madly in love with him.

One day, she notices the man with a woman – his girlfriend. In a fit of rage, the agoraphobic bangs on the window, miming threats and provoking their attention. The couple knocks angrily on the woman's door. She's terrified – the outside world is trying to come in! – and the police turn up.

Conversations take place through her mail slot. The cop confirms to this flawed but scared woman that the world indeed is an overflowing toilet of festering grief. However, it's also an amazing place worth taking the risk for. The film ends with the woman unlocking the door and opening her world to a potential fresh start.

While hardly something to lead an Academy Awards speech, the story features only one location and four cast members. In fact, the cop's dialogue could actually be spoken by the love interest actor … so maybe don't hire a Playgirl model for that role.

Point is, this story of a woman overcoming fear is short, simple, and easy as pie to film. Express big ideas in the most minimal way possible, and you'll be sure to keep your story out of the slush pile.

Homework
Task 1
Bingewatch

Sitting comfortably? It's time to get a numb butt and put some serious hours into watching – remember, it's part of your education. You're going to learn all about micro-budgets and large budgets and why sometimes a bigger budget doesn't make a better movie.

- Watch a gargantuan budget movie. We suggest *Bright* ($90 million) or *Avengers Infinity War* ($321 million).
- Then watch *The Florida Project* ($2 million) or *The Blair Witch Project* ($60k).
- Bear in mind in Hollywood $15 million is considered "low-budget", so $2 million is micro-budget.
- Get out your notepad and scribble some observations.
- In the low-budget movies, note the use of locations to keep costs down.
- Note the number of actors and special effects used in each movie.
- Ask yourself at the end: was I gripped? Did I enjoy that movie?

Task 2
Think of your script as a micro-budget movie

This task will give you an idea of the limitations filmmakers and screenwriters face when their projects go into production and help you focus on infusing the narrative structure with a strong sense of story.

- Think of your current script project as a micro-budget movie.
- Think about locations you have access to and adapt your screenplay around these locations.
- Think about how much your movie would cost to shoot.
- Create a mock budget, keeping costs as low as possible.

Extra Credit

Would your working movie title work regardless of the budget? Why so or why not?

8.
Make research your BFF,
pt. 2

We're back with your one and only source on how to write a screenplay in 30 days. Now you know how to get inspired – and how to ensure your artistic genius is filmable – we're bringing you back to the books again to reemphasize a super important subject: research.

Say you're writing a drama about an investigative journalist, but have exactly zero experience in the field. The best way to find out? Take a big swig of coffee, lean back in your writing chair, and fire an email to one. Explain that you're fascinated by her work and want to write an authentic story about someone just like her.

This type of ballsy approach is just the sort of unusual request that piques the interest of people. Once you specify you're working on a film or TV script and need their help with it, they can immediately envision themselves onscreen and may want to participate. You'll be surprised how helpful people can be when asked.

Some writers have even been along on drug busts with the police, gone into the field with the army, and casually hung out in sex dungeons. These writers produce highly realistic scripts because they spent time in the shoes of their subjects. They've soaked up the same atmosphere, experienced the emotions, and witnessed the same notable moments.

When putting pen to paper, they rarely suffer from writer's block, because of a springboard of stories, dialogue, moments, and emotions saved up and waiting in their notebooks.

If you want to write a screenplay, you probably already possess a love for writing dialogue. Imagine how much more fun you'll have once the lines feel absolutely real to you. You'll already know all your characters' quirks, responses, and inflections, having experienced them all first hand.

Go the extra mile for your script and interview the people on the periphery of your subject – the supporting players to populate the outskirts of your story universe.

Coming back to the concept for your gritty reporter drama: you could also interview people who have worked with that journalist: editors, photographers, even the people who were subjects of one of their stories. Ask them how they worked with the journalist, what they did, and why. Take notes not just on *what* they say, but *how* they say it.

Doing your own research is what makes your world deep and real. You may be thinking, "My cosmic horror opera is set in the future on a planet that doesn't exist, so this does not concern me." You might not be able to visit your planet, but you can still explore the characters by finding similar individuals from everyday reality. You might not know any alien saxophonists, but a human one can still offer interesting details.

If you need extra inspiration, check out the work of documentarian Louis Theroux. Take notes on the questions he asks his interviewees and how they respond. Theroux has a distinct way of making even his most antagonistic subjects so comfortable that they share intimate personal information on camera.

That's the juicy research apple you're climbing the tree for: if you want that ripe fruit, you can't just shake the trunk and hope it falls. Sometimes, you have to climb carefully to retrieve the most vital parts of your story.

Typing up that exciting first draft of your script undoubtedly forms the bulk of your writing, but discovery dwells in its heart. Keep that heart healthy by being adventurous – and thorough – with your research.

Homework
Task 1

Here's a Trello Board to help you with contributor research.

```
https://trello.com/b/v69PlGez/from-zero-to-hero-contributor-template
```

- Return to your research folder / Trello board / Evernote.
- Is anything else you can add to it?
- Are there any other people you could interview?
- Research who your characters are.
- Find actors (doesn't matter how famous) who fit the description of your character.
- Move on with your research to a more visual stage:
- Make a Pinterest board with the headshots of your chosen actors …
- and another with pictures of locations similar to the ones you want to use in your script, in order to paint a clearer image of your visual story.
- Think of all your research as your raw and unrefined screenplay.
- This work contains all the answers and information related to your screenplay.

Task 2

- Compile a reading and watch list around the topic you are writing on.
- Explore as many avenues as you possibly can: travel books, biographies, documentaries.
- Visit as many of your desired locations as you can. Experiencing places physically will help you dramatically when imagining your scenes taking place.
- If you haven't already, reach out to professionals relevant to subjects in your script. Authenticity is rarely seen in amateur scripts, so get your script to the top of the pile with this research technique.

Extra credit

Do a web search for the most successful movies of all time. What do you learn from their movie titles?

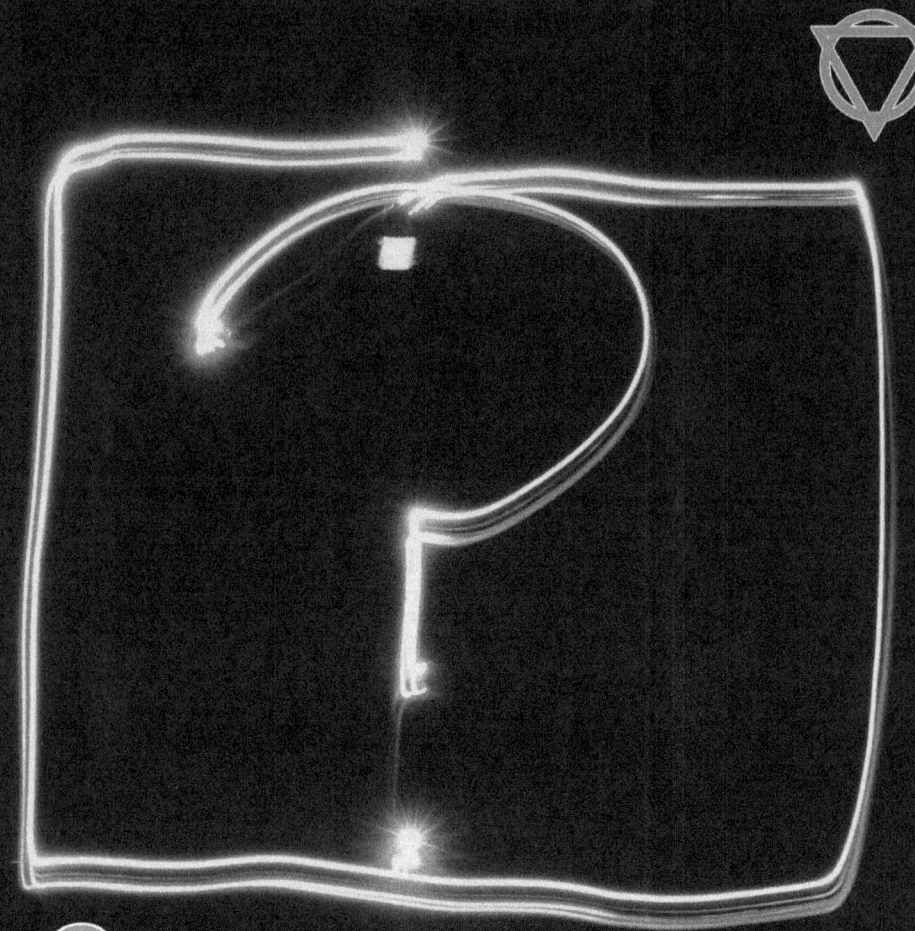

9.
WTF is genre, anyway?

When someone asks you what your film is about, how will you introduce it? Is it a thriller, a comedy, horror, romance, or – lord help us – a bromance?

Genre is important, and is one of the first things people respond to. You can know whether you want to see a movie within seconds of seeing its promotional poster.

You might know it's a comedy from the goofy expressions worn by the actors, or a science fiction movie from the starfield background and futuristic gadgets. Every element, from the title and tagline to the fonts and colors chosen, is designed to advertise a specific film genre to maximize revenue by targeting the exact demographic willing to spend money on it.

Granted, a short film like yours may not require an elaborate poster, but the concept remains the same. Imagine you want to watch a comedy, because you need a break from trying to figure out your new screenplay's genre. Based on its movie poster, you opt for a zany-looking workplace comedy in which a hapless employee is at odds with his arrogant boss.

You settle into the movie theater and await the euphoria of laughter. But the second act's humorless tragedy shows this ain't no comedy. You were hoodwinked by a fun poster – this is a harrowing drama.

Genre is important. It forms the foundations upon which your story's entire edifice rests. Set it up poorly, and your structure could crumble into ruins. Choose wisely and get an unshakable marvel you can build on with confidence.

It's crucial to decide where on the genre scale your script sits: to ensure your movie hits the right beats – or subverts them in a shrewd, masterful way – you'll need to understand your genre inside and out.

Watch *everything* you can in that genre, and study those films intently. Keep written notes on exactly what connects pieces to their genres.

By doing so, you'll climb higher atop the mountain of your story. You might even find yourself spotting aspects of movies you've encountered in others before – even a movie you're too cool to admit to your friends you've seen a hundred and twelve times.

Your new mission, should you choose to accept it, is to enjoy films in a new way, a different way than mass audiences.

Understand why a film evokes tears, laughter, gasps, and screams. Analyze the craft of the writing and the other skills employed to draw these responses. Make a note of all the conventions used to create these impactful moments, and familiarize yourself with your genre's most common tropes.

Ever noticed how sitcoms always have an idiot or a fall guy?

- Charlie in It's Always Sunny in Philadelphia
- Dinesh in *Silicon Valley*
- Jason in *The Good Place*
- Jerry in *Rick and Morty*

You'll also find a character with a questionable moral compass:

- Dennis in *It's Always Sunny in Philadelphia*
- Gavin Belson in *Silicon Valley*
- Michael in *The Good Place*
- Rick in *Rick and Morty*

Horror films are famous for their tropes: the creepy location where someone was brutally murdered in the past; the fake-out jump scare in which a sudden noise is actually caused by a harmless raccoon or a floorboard; the gratuitous sex scene leading directly to violent murder.

Once you understand your genre's assumed elements, you can decide whether those tropes belong in your film. If you're feeling even more confident with a particular genre, you may even want to play with convention a little.

At The CW teen show *Riverdale*'s heart, for example, is a typical teen drama adhering to the usual rules. But it's also a smart exercise in genre-mashing, featuring elements of horror, Lynchian surrealism, and gee-whiz Americana.

The writers only know when and how to play with tropes because they know the genres inside and out.

Quentin Tarantino is another master of genre-bending films that deliver on expectations, but also subvert them. Tarantino can only break the rules because he's an insufferable film nerd who knows his genres meticulously. It's about playing with your audience's expectations of the common tropes and surprising them with a twist.

Genre is important: decide on yours and take the time to become a true expert, because once you're its master, you're in complete control. Use those newly acquired powers to explore classic tropes – or provide a fresh twist on your genre – and you'll have a dynamite screenplay in the making.

Homework

Task 1
Resurrect your creativity in your dead time

You're feeling pretty darn great with yourself right now, the lessons have been enlightening, and you're flying through this homework like a crazy person. We're going to ask a little more of you this time, which involves some studying: some *real* homework!

- We know you're hella busy! Work, college, kids, social life, needy pets! We recommend you come up with a nifty little schedule made up of short pieces to watch in your genre. On the bus? Dead time, my friend! Even if it's a 10-minute journey, you can squeeze in a little short film. Make a schedule to fill all the little pockets of dead time in your life. Does your partner hog the bathroom for half an hour every night? That's an episode of TV right there!
- Compile a list of TV shows and shorts to watch on your favorite online streaming service whenever and wherever you can. Note all the tropes and conventions you find.
- Can't get your head around the concept of tropes? Bookmark this baby as *the* in-depth essential resource. (Warning: don't get lost down the rabbit hole!) https://tvtropes.org/

Task 2
Genre genius – make Tarantino blush

- Make a genre document or add to your Evernote mindmap, making sure to include things like its history, pioneers, etc.
- Become an EXPERT of that genre – know it like the back of your hand.

Extra credit

Does your movie title work with the genre of movie you are writing? Why so or why not? If it doesn't fit into your genre then maybe start rethinking your title.

10.
Augment your craft with the best tech tools.

You have a bombass story idea. You've sweated through all that painstaking research. You've stared into space and spun around on your office chair for at least an hour between bursts of productivity. And now you're ready to start typing up your first draft.

You open up Microsoft Word and... Microsoft Word? Seriously?!

The painful truth is there is nothing worse than a screenplay in Word. They're hard to read and more importantly, they look amateurish. So what are the alternatives that won't break the bank?

Final Draft is the industry standard, but it costs over $200. If you happen to have Scrooge McDuck volumes of loose change in your couch, it may be a worthwhile investment.

For a more basic choice without the many detailed functions of Final Draft, Celtx is an affordable alternative. It's free on Windows and cheap on the App Store. Celtx helps with formatting, collaboration, and even storyboarding. If you want to get more advanced, Celtx offers paid expansion packs.

Maybe you crave access to your screenplay at all times. Out on a terrible, yet oddly inspirational, date? Supposed to be working your day job? There are also screenwriting apps for your phone or tablet.

Both Final Draft and Celtx offer versions for your phone, but we also recommend: WriterDuet, perfect for screenwriting collaboration; Scripts Peo, the best-reviewed screenwriting app, also compatible with Final Draft and Celtx; Untitled, terrific for turning scrappy notes into a screenplay; and Slugline: Simply Screenwriting, a straightforward choice similar to Final Draft.

With these tools at your disposal, your dazzler of a screenplay won't be burdened by unprofessional formatting errors.

Ready for the next step of your journey? Throw on your most heroic clothes (or at least some clean sweats) because in the next lesson, we'll be exploring the legendary Hero's Journey.

Homework

Here's a neat little list of everything we mentioned earlier, so you don't have to scroll through the whole lesson again – we're good to you, aren't we? Now, get cracking!

Task 1
Desktop delicacies

Here are the computer screenwriting tools you can check out for yourself:

- **Final Draft 10**: $299.99
  Current industry standard
- **Celtx** (basic): FREE (approx. $19.99 through the App Store)
  Most-used software, due to its industry contending features & price.

Task 2
For the small screen wordsmiths

Here are the mobile screenwriting apps we recommend:

- **Final Draft**: in-app purchase for full use
- **Celtx**: FREE
- **WriterDuet** - FREE
  Rumored to be slowly overtaking Final Draft as the industry favorite
- **Scripts Pro**: approx. $19.99
  Highly reviewed, contending app; compatible with Final Draft & Celtx
- **Slugline: Simply Screenwriting**: approx. $39.99
  Nothing substantially differentiated from the others, but worth checking out

You will soon discover what works best for you. Good luck!

Extra credit

Ruminate on your movie title. You should be happy with your choice – but remember that you can always change it.

11.
What's a logline got to do with it?

To logline, or not to logline, that is the question. Or maybe the real question is: what in the name of Lynch is a logline, anyway?

Simply put, a logline is a marketing tool for agents and producers to get a feel for a piece quickly. A good logline can sell your script to that studio fat cat, while a bad one may be used to light his cigar.

A logline should be taut and punchy, expressing the essentials of your story. Check out these two loglines that are so good you should immediately recognize the movies they're selling:

A clownfish, afraid of the ocean, is forced to leave his Great Barrier Reef to swim through unknown territory and rescue his captured son in Sydney.

A powerful but arrogant god is cast out of Asgard to live among humans on Earth, where he soon becomes one of their most valuable defenders.

Why do these loglines work so well? A single sentence shows us a protagonist, a world, a journey, and a complication.

A producer needs solid loglines like these to sell a project in one sentence to his busy corporate pals. Is your project too hard to condense into a single sentence? Then maybe its story is too complicated for your audience to understand.

Want to hear a really awful logline?

Once upon a time, there was a little girl who went by the name of Sarah and she was always really nice to everyone and nothing ever bothered her.

It may be obvious why this one sucks so hard, but let's dive in anyways. Firstly, too much has been given away with this logline. Want to reel that hotshot producer in? Leave her wanting more!

Secondly, there's no drama whatsoever. Sarah sounds like a total snooze who couldn't find conflict if it stabbed her in the throat. She's *nice*. Nothing bothers her. We're asleep already.

Lastly, it's utterly lacking a world, journey, or complication. For all we know, Sarah's entire story is staring out a window for fifteen minutes. Why should anyone care?

Try this logline instead:

A Los Angeles undercover cop must decide where his loyalties lie when he gets seduced by the street-racing underworld he came to expose.

We can imagine the handsome, bombastic lead. We get what's eating our hero and why he has to act. We know the setting, so we understand the context and we can suspend disbelief. We see the guns, fast cars, and maybe even cinematic explosions in case of street-racing mishaps.

Loglines are important. They're the delicate gift wrapping of your script – are you going to tie your story with an irresistible bow a producer can't help but tug open? Or are you going to dump it in a trash bag and hope for the best? The choice is yours.

Homework

A budding screenwriter faces the trials of loglines, only to find it's much more fun than she originally thought.

Task 1
These are the loglines you're looking for

- Go on IMDB and click on a bunch of movies and TV shows.
- Notice that each and every one contains a logline near the top.
- Write out the loglines for twenty to thirty films / TV shows so you can get that succinct style under your fingers.

Task 2
Who said writing lines was a punishment?

Write a logline for your idea. Can you sum it up in a sentence? If not, the chances are the story won't work later on in the writing process.

Look at your logline, then look at the list of professional loglines from Task 1. Are they structured in the same way? Is yours too long?

Try this with some like-minded friends; read them out to each other. Make it fun! You can help each other make them great – plus it's great practice.

Next step

It's time! Open up your screenwriting software and create your title page. Your title page needs to include – you guessed it! – your slick movie title.

It also needs to include:

- Your name (or nom de plume)
- Your e-mail address
- Your phone number

Keep your title page simple like this – no one is impressed by artistic covers – they just look like you're trying to cover up a poor script with glitter & sparkles.

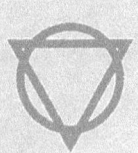

12.
Find your voice – and stick with it.

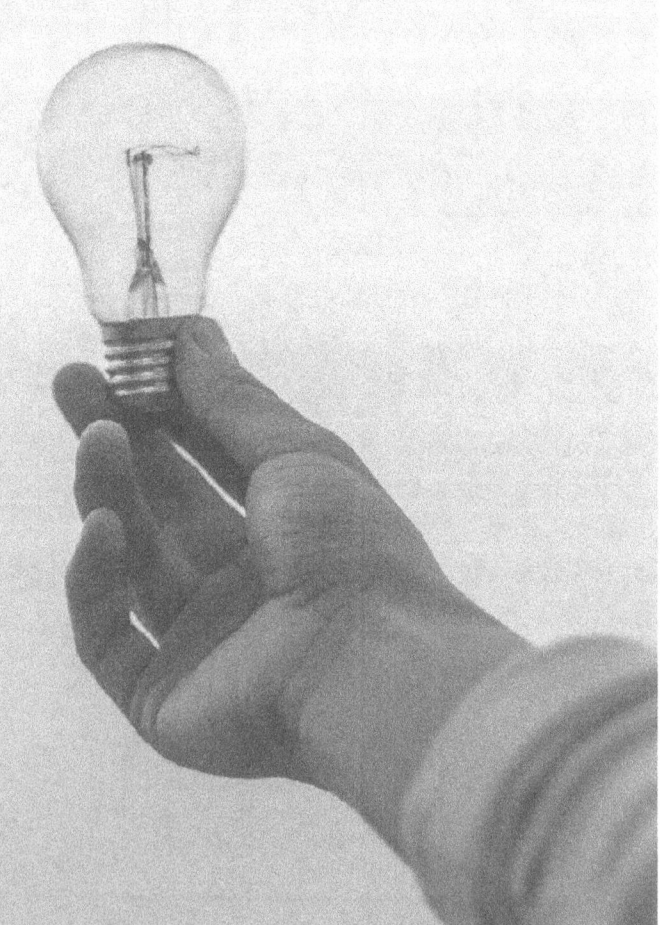

Get some wine on ice, dim the lights, and throw on that one Drake song that makes you feel fuzzy in a special place, because we're going to set some serious mood.

No, we're not gonna drop the smoothest sex-ed video the world has ever seen. Get ready for the smoothest screenwriting lesson about the voice of your script ever.

Like the dulcet voices of the sexiest-ever love songs, the voice of your screenplay sets the tone of your overall joint.

When it comes to storytelling, tone is the incredibly important core emotion you want the audience to feel. Don't dilly-dally; jump on that pony and establish your tone *right away*. The audience needs to know what emotions they're in for.

Maybe it's a social realism piece, full of grit; a dark, brooding horror with an air of romance; or a lighthearted comedy that's actually horny as hell. All can be expressed perfectly in your very first image.

An opening shot about death very clearly establishes a particular mood. A jaunty romcom won't open with this shot, but a horror certainly can.

By now you should know what story you want to tell, and why you want to tell it. What emotion does that story evoke?

The visceral emotion you feel deep down is the *single most important element* of the entire writing process.

That emotion is your primary tone. It is also your voice – the one that drags you away from parties & procrastination, and pulls you to press on with the story and ensure you'll be heard.

How do you want the audience to feel while reading or watching your work? Capture that emotion. Stick it in your writing pantry, then pull it out and sprinkle it all over your script.

Once you know your voice, stick to it. If you break that carefully crafted tone, you'll leave the audience confused and feeling betrayed that you didn't deliver on the mood you promised at the outset. Nobody likes a tease.

Tone vibes off both genre and themes, so it can be convenient to decide all three at the same time.

Imagine your movie is a macabre comedy about a woman who attends her own funeral from beyond the grave. Your genre is "black comedy", your tone is "dark humor", and your main theme is "death". A cogent screenplay's genre, tone, and themes always work in tandem.

Tones and genres come with specific expectations and rule sets. In *The Walking Dead*, for example, the rules concern regular people in a very *irregular* world. You wouldn't expect Rick to rock a slapstick dance number while running away from a zombie horde, or Michonne to try out new jokes for her standup act for an entire episode.

Those would be ludicrous shifts in tone, compromising our belief in the story and its characters. In turn, we might no longer be able to suspend our disbelief in this madcap story. Instead, *The Walking Dead* has maintained the same tone and mood throughout the series – and you should seek to do the same. Don't confuse your tone, and you won't confuse your audience.

Throw on that song that inspires you, light some candles, set some serious mood – and stay on that track. Finding the right balance between theme, genre, and tone is the sexy scent that gives your script swagger and stability. Let your voice be heard!

Homework

You guessed it – you get to watch more stuff. We know – we're just so horrible to you! Get your notepad and pen ready and prepare yourself for some active watching.

Goooood . . . let the voice flow through you

Watch a few films or TV shows. In the first few scenes of each, observe the tone presented.

For example in the very first episode of *Riverdale*, there is a death almost immediately, which sets the tone for the show. Now we know this show will be very serious at times – we know what tone to expect, what we're in for.

In your chosen films and TV shows, note how quickly the tone is set, and *how* it is set.

Extra credit

Look over your title page and make sure you're still happy with it.

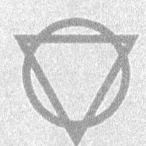

13.
The hero's journey in 5 minutes

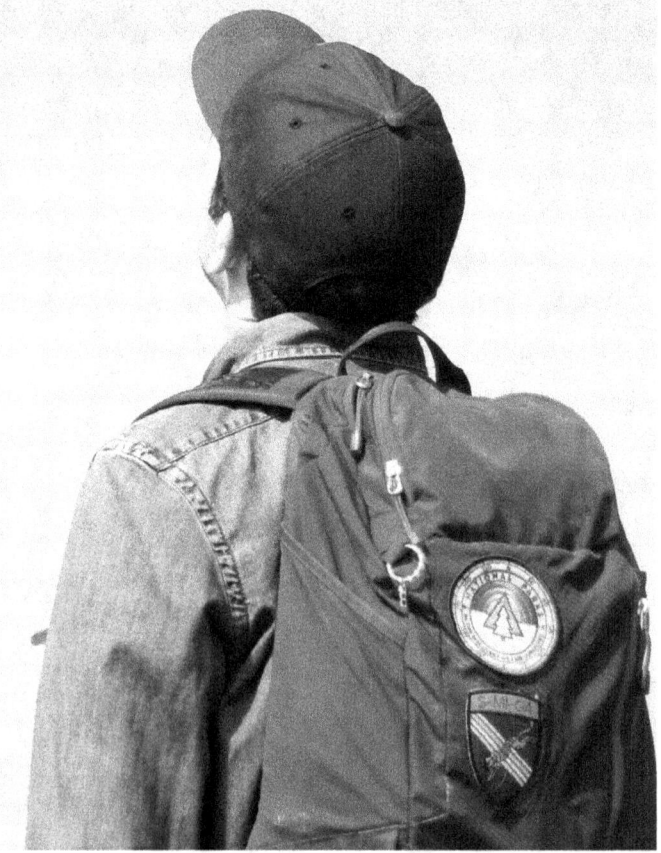

No matter what your story is about or where it's set, your screenplay has to be about *someone*. Between its start and end, this person must also experience a so-called "journey of change".

It sounds like something a college freshman says after spending two days in India – but it's also one of the oldest storytelling rules.

To go on this journey, the protagonist must be flawed in some way. During the course of the story, the character discovers this flaw, strives to fix it, and returns transformed, victorious.

Basically, your character's primary flaw is also her primary *need*.

When we meet the protagonist, it should be evident she's a hot mess because of this particular need – of which she appears completely unaware.

Maybe she's a scumbag billionaire who learns to value people over material wealth, or he's a new father who, before raising a child well, must first grow up himself.

Think about your script and lead character. She has a need she'll assimilate through the course of the story – but can't simply discover it, fix it, and get on with her life immediately.

Write *that* lackluster story and you may have another Titanic on your hands: the ship, not the movie. We mean it'll sink to the bottom of your storytelling ocean, never to host another shindig in third class again.

Here's what you do instead: make your character *want* something. Make her want something so much she's steaming at the ears and dribbling all over the syntax of your script. But here's where you switch it up: the character has to think she can only find happiness upon achieving this desire.

It is acquiring what she *needs* – not merely what she wants – that actually completes her.

In *Colossal*, for instance, we follow Anne Hathaway's Gloria, a party girl whose inner demons impact the world in a terrifying and inexplicable way as she manifests as a Kaiju monster in Seoul, Korea. We're introduced to Gloria, drunk and being kicked out by her boyfriend, and assume she can only find happiness if she grows up, gets sober, and sorts her life out.

Though sobriety is a solid goal for Gloria, what she actually *needs* is autonomy and empowerment. Like the monster she's unwittingly controlling, Gloria has to take control of herself and her actions. The character *wants* sobriety –

but *needs* self-possession.

In the first season of the Netflix Originals series *GLOW*, Alison Brie's antihero Ruth thinks landing a "respectable" acting career is the only thing that will bring her happiness. As the story progresses, it becomes clear that Ruth, who has been sabotaging herself in a myriad of ways – including boning her best friend's husband – *needs* the stability, support, and steady employment that the women's wrestling league provides her.

Ruth *wants* the Hollywood dream, but *needs* to embrace her Hollywood reality.

Dan Harmon, writer and creator of *Rick and Morty* and *Community*, explains the hero's journey in eight simple steps:

1. A character is in a zone of comfort.
2. But she wants something.
3. She enters an unfamiliar situation.
4. She adapts to it.
5. She gets what she wanted.
6. But she pays a heavy price for it.
7. She returns to her familiar situation.
8. But she's changed as a result of her experience.

When crafting your story, ask yourself, "What will my character learn through this journey of change?"

Before you write *anything* – even a title – know the answer to that question. You'll need it to survive the gauntlet of our next lesson, which concerns the structure and essential beats of your story.

Homework

You're about to witness first-hand how a character's want and need are the secret to storytelling. Without these two seemingly simple ideas, you have no story – So don't go skipping this homework!

Task 1
You want to write. You need discipline.

Come up with a *need* for your protagonist. Now come up with something they *want* badly.

You have come up with the back bone to your story. This is what will be driving your character from start to finish.

Watch your favorite film. (This task is easier when it's a film you know well). Identify the protagonist's want and need and see how they relate to each other.

Do this with everything you watch. It's good practice to train yourself to think in this way about stories.

Task 2
Going in circles – not a bad thing?

Once you've completed Task 1, apply Dan Harmon's story structure theory to it:

Storytelling comes naturally to humans, but since we live in an unnatural world, we sometimes need a little help doing what we'd naturally do.

Draw a circle and divide it in half vertically. Divide the circle again horizontally.

Starting from the 12 o'clock position and going clockwise, number the 4 points where the lines cross the circle: 1, 3, 5 and 7. Number the quarter-sections themselves 2, 4, 6 and 8."

DAY 13

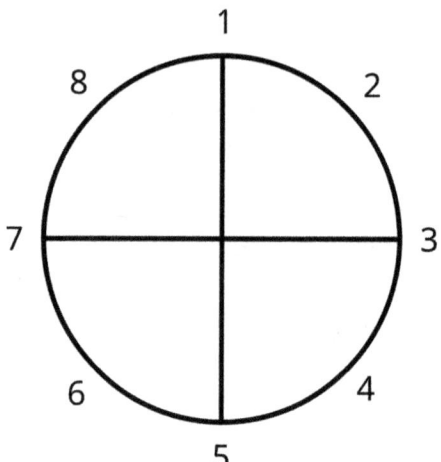

1. A character is in a zone of comfort
2. But she wants something
3. She enters an unfamiliar situation
4. Adapts to it
5. Gets what she wanted
6. Pays a heavy price for it
7. Then returns to her familiar situation
8. Having changed

Extra credit

Add your logline to your title page.

14.
Beginning, middle, and end . . . not always in that order

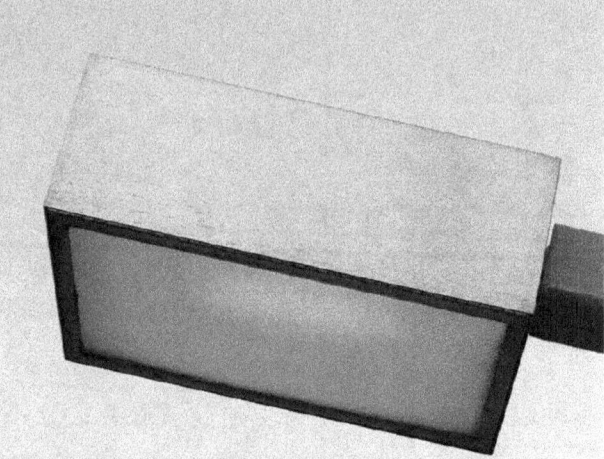
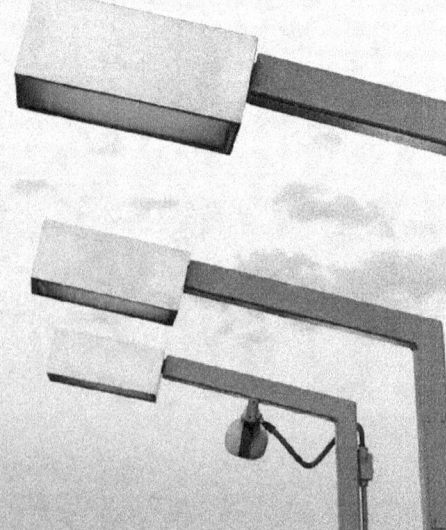

You've probably been aware of the importance of story structure since you were little. It starts with a bold setup, providing the lowdown of key characters and setting:

> *Once upon a time in a military facility far, far away, there was a scared amphibian man locked in a tank, and a lonely cleaning woman who cleaned his room.*

You know there has to be a middle part involving a confrontation:

> *Over time, the cleaning lady and the amphibian man fell in love. She hatched a plan to break him out and save him – but the evil colonel of the facility did everything in his power to stop them!*

Then, there's the climax of happily-ever-after:

> *After a tense showdown on the waterfront, the amphibian man and the cleaning woman defeated the evil colonel and swam off to live a life of bliss together under the waves.*

or unhappily-ever-after, if you're feeling edgy:

> *The amphibian man was killed by the evil colonel, who ruled the facility with an iron fist forevermore. The cleaning woman barely escaped, taking the lessons of her first love with her.*

This is the classic three-act structure every beginning drama student learns – but you'd be surprised how many scripts fail because they don't have a clear beginning, middle, and end. Think of it as the simple everyday recipe by which you'll learn how to cook up a great script. So let's break down all the essentials of this dish.

Act One: The succulent setup

A lot of ingredients are juggled in the first act. This is the place where the audience becomes acquainted with your protagonist (flaws and all), along with the other key players in the story. The antagonist is also introduced in Act One with the potential threats he, she, or it poses to the hero.

The location and time period in which the story takes place should be established, and crucial story components like genre, tone, and overall themes must be set up. Other plot points may also be introduced, primarily in relation to the main character arcs.

All these ingredients should be expressed as visually – and sparingly – as possible. Don't pull a *Suicide Squad* by overstuffing your opening with five introductions for each character. Less is more – especially when writing a short film. Say as much as you can in as few words as possible.

Once the setup is complete, we're ready for something major to happen: the *inciting incident*. The inciting incident can take any form – it can be as big or as small as the story requires, but its conflict must force the protagonist into the decision to act. This is the moment that pushes him to leave his familiar world for new challenges.

In *Rocky*, world heavyweight boxing champion Apollo Creed challenges Rocky Balboa to a match the down-on-his-luck fighter only has a million-to-one shot to win. In *Star Wars*, Luke Skywalker's aunt and uncle are savagely slaughtered by Imperial stormtroopers, leaving Luke without a family on his home planet.

In light of the inciting incident, the hero is left with no choice but to leave his comfort zone and is propelled into action as we're hurled into the uncharted waters of Act Two.

Act Two: The mouthwatering middle

The script moves on to the meat of the story as your protagonist starts on a new mission. In Act Two, he encounters a string of obstacles which must be overcome in pursuit of his goal – where he fights to achieve the things he wants and needs.

During the first half of Act Two, the protagonist is completely invested in obtaining his goal – the thing he *wants*. At this stage, he may not even be aware of what he *needs*, as he experiments but still can't comprehend deeply his requirement to change. The audience is led to believe the only thing of importance to the main character is what he wants.

Eventually, the protagonist's need becomes an overpowering force too visible to ignore: this forms the *midpoint* of your script – the crux of the Hero's Journey. For the first time in the story, the protagonist's needs are portrayed as more substantial to his journey than what he wanted at the start.

To put it another way, the midpoint accentuates the true values of the protagonist – what is and what isn't important to him – in a way that's clear to the audience, so they're invested in the emotional journey of the hero.

We see that Rocky Balboa lacks inner self-worth (his need), but is too invested in the opportunity to show his worth publicly against the heavyweight champion (his want). The midpoint scene occurs after gym owner Mickey – who ignored Rocky in the past – offers to train him, and Rocky angrily rejects him.

In *Star Wars*, Luke Skywalker is happy being Obi-Wan Kenobi's jedi apprentice (his want), but circumstances require him to step up and be a hero (his need). The midpoint occurs when Luke resolves to rescue Princess Leia.

The midpoint presents a massive marker of change in the hero; nothing will be the same from this point onwards. This event is often accentuated by literal or metaphorical acts of sex or death. Whatever your protagonist does at this transformative breakthrough *must* be something he was unable to do at the start of the story.

After the big moment of the midpoint comes a major misstep: something that proves the protagonist still has lessons to learn. Though he's made progress, he still hasn't undergone a full character transformation yet. The hero is unable to think things through properly, and therefore experiences a setback on his journey.

Although he stood up to Mickey, Rocky's misstep is failing to stand up to his friend Paulie, who takes advantage of him by inviting a journalist to film Rocky training. In *Star Wars*, Luke's misstep is bungling Leia's rescue, risking their lives cornered in a shootout. In fact, Leia herself is forced to take the lead, grabbing a blaster and effecting their escape through the garbage chute.

After this misstep, the protagonist realizes there's still a lot to learn. He doubts his ability to take what he's learned so far and conquer the antagonist, so he regresses back to his unchanged self. This is the *point of lost hope*: the audience is made to believe the hero could genuinely fail against the villain.

Once the goal seems firmly out of reach, the protagonist is finally able to experience a key epiphany: his *need* is of primary significance. This revelation is a critical marker of permanent change for our hero, and it can take many forms. A side character could give a rousing speech that prompts the hero to inhabit his new self fully and defeat the villain; or, a violent act could provoke him to transform and conquer the antagonist.

The protagonist has experienced his point of lost hope and pulled himself from the brink of failure. Now that he's also been hit with this major revelation, he actively chooses to step totally into the shoes of his new identity. The hero is reborn from the ashes of his failure stronger, wiser, and clear-sighted enough to face the villain for the final showdown.

But the hero simply *deciding* to take action isn't enough to propel the plot forward to Act Three. He must be shown actually *taking* the action, which forms the *second act turning point*. What it entails is up to you and depends on your plot. It could be your hero slapping the villain with a wet fish and challenging him to a duel. Or, it could be the character facing his fear of water to jump in a sailboat and save his friends. Whatever it is thrusts Act Three into motion.

Act Three: The full-bodied flourish

From the moment the hero takes that first step towards his big battle against the antagonist, the beginning of the sweet, sweet climax has begun. The story forms a crescendo from here, building up to the emotional peak when the primary antagonist is defeated – or not, as the case may be.

This climactic battle signals the end of the protagonist's journey of change, as he leverages his newfound persona to defeat the antagonist. The climax embodies the *point* of – the meaning behind – your story, towards which every plot element so far has been driving. Even if your hero loses against the antagonist, he must still master his inner need.

The climax must be the most consequential and exciting part of your story. This cathartic and satisfying conflict gives the audience the emotional culmination that they've been waiting for. Make yours memorable!

The climax in *Rocky* is of course the big boxing match between Apollo and Rocky. In *Star Wars*, it's a literal war among the stars, as Luke and the Rebellion take on the villainous Darth Vader and his Death Star battle station.

After this peak showdown comes the protagonist's Total Mastery, confirmation that the hero has undergone a complete inner change to master his new identity. The Total Mastery may even provide him the opportunity to tie up other loose ends from the journey.

In *Star Wars*, Luke's Total Mastery is on display when he returns from having destroyed the Death Star and restored hope to the galaxy – replete with cheesy award ceremony. Rocky's moment of Total Mastery arrives just after the boxing match ends, as he cries out for the woman who loves him, totally ignoring the crowd around him surging with expectation to learn the fight's winner (which is actually Apollo).

If at all possible, avoid having your protagonist *explain* how he's achieved Total Mastery. Instead, find a way to *show* he's changed by devising the best action to highlight the character's permanent transformation.

Total Mastery forms the denouement of the story, tending to make up the final minutes of a movie; it provides closure to the audience by conclusively resolving the protagonist's character arc.

Last thoughts

Form can obviously be flexible, and filmmakers like David Lynch and Quentin Tarantino are renowned for playing with the traditional linear three acts of storytelling; regardless, their films still possess structure.

Revisit your favorite movies and deconstruct them based on the basic storytelling principles of the three-act form. The best movies feature all the hallmarks of great structure, but in such a subtle way that the changes feel seamless and inevitable.

Want to work some sleight-of-hand into your script with a classic insider tip? Prepare your midpoint, climax, and Total Mastery before you even begin to write, and the rest of the recipe will fall right into place.

Homework

Time to pick apart your favourite films or TV shows, ruining them for yourself completely! Just kidding – you'll enjoy them in a whole new way. When you're watching with a buddy, just sit in a cloud of your own smugness, knowing exactly why your friend is enjoying this certain scene so much.

Enjoy unravelling your enjoyment

In a few of your favourite movies/shows, identify:

- the inciting incident
- the midpoint and how it is marked by sex or death (literally or metaphorically)
- the act breaks
- the Total Mastery scenes at the end

Some easy movies to spot structure like the above are Disney movies.

Next step

Shape your story into the three-act structure outlined in this lesson.

So you've found your story, discovered your muse, figured out the character arc of your protagonist, worked out a theme, decided on your story's tone and genre, and done all that crucial research.

Unleash your maniacal laugh, because it's time to get plotting. Pick up a boatload of index cards, as you're going to be turning the wall of your workstation into your movie. Blake Snyder, the dude who wrote *Save the Cat*, calls this a "beat sheet".

There are actually several types of beats, but for this lesson we'll explore plot beats. Plot beats are units of action that make up your story.

First, on a regular sheet of paper – or your computer or your iPad or your phone – write down a summary of your plot as a list of beats, using only one or two sentences per beat – keep each plot beat as succinct as possible.

Once the list is done, take an index card or your preferred digital tool for each beat. Start each card with the slugline for the scene, like "`INT. CAFETERIA – DAY`", then add a one- or two-sentence description of the scene's action.

Keep the cards as terse as possible – feel free to be subjective. Each card exists to provide you a clear overview of your story at every step, allowing you to identify scenes without having to trawl through a minefield of words.

Next, take four cards for the essential stages of your story's structure: Act 1, Act 2A, Act 2B, and Act 3. Place each plot beat card in chronological order next to its corresponding act card. Ensure that you end each act with a card containing the dramatic turning point that catapults the story into the next act.

Act 1 ends shortly after your inciting incident; Act 2A ends with the midpoint card; and Act 2B ends at the moment the character gets ballsy and takes on the antagonist.

If the words written on the acts' final cards don't make your palms sweaty, your heart race, and your hair raise, rethink why you're settling for anything less than that.

A beat sheet provides a simple point of reference describing when events occur, in order to visualize your movie as a whole and save you from constantly having to comb through your script. Think that violent diner scene works better as the inciting incident, rather than the midpoint card? Move those cards around and shake up the flow of your story.

The beat sheet is a great way to track subplots. Highlight all the scenes featuring that awesome subplot involving the gangster's cocaine-loving wife, so you can get a good feel for its balance throughout the movie.

All screenwriters use some variation of this beat-organizing technique, as it's a vital way to stay on top of the scene flow and the dynamic changes of your story. So pin those cards on your wall and see your movie take form.

Your next challenge: how are you going to *tell* this bomb-ass story?

Homework

You're about to embark on the fun part – the part when you turn all those scrappy notes, your research folder, and whatever else you have into actual scenes. That wall in your room is gonna look mighty pretty when you're finished with it!

Just beat it!

- Buy some 3x5" index cards and write your beats on them.
- Clear a big space on your wall.
- Beat out your story.
- Remember: keep the summaries MINIMAL.
- Alternative: if you're more of a web person, use Trello instead.

Next step

Write "`FADE IN:`" in your screenplay document, then write the opening image to your story – just the opening image. Consider:

- Whom do we see first?
- What is the tone?
- What do we want our audience to think?
- What do we want our audience to feel?

16. Dialogue that kills

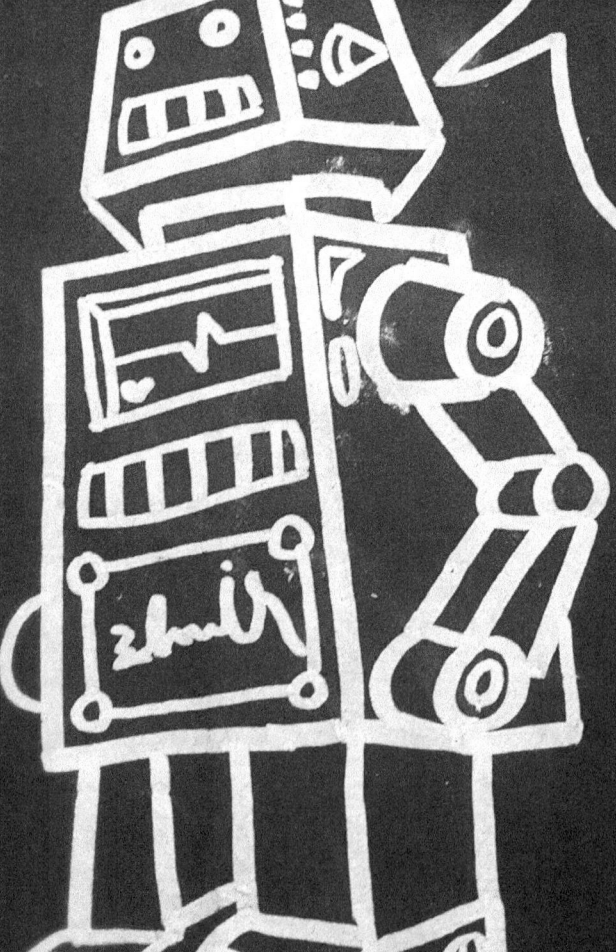

Ready to write dialogue so sharp it'll rip through the pages of your script? If you have an enthusiasm for dialogue, one of the first things you're likely to do is develop your characters by giving them vocal cues you think bring them to life.

We're here to tell you to resist that urge.

Though dialogue certainly helps reveal character and moves the story forward, it's something to add in at the final stage of your story, coming only after you've figured out your genre and Hero's Journey, plotted out the entire script, and cobbled together your beat sheet.

Dialogue also requires balance and moderation. A common mistake of new writers is writing too much dialogue, putting everyone to sleep by the third page. The first thing to remember when writing dialogue is that you're writing for a visual medium. Pictures can carry a lot of exposition.

Wasting pages on long-winded conversations and Shakespearean soliloquies may seem captivating to you, but if the dialogue doesn't push the story forward or provide relevant insights to each character, pound that delete key pronto.

Think of dialogue as the hot sauce of your script. In fact, think of it as the hottest sauce imaginable – pure fire that could kill a man if handled improperly. Use it only when absolutely necessary.

Dialogue is often used as a way for characters to hide their true emotions, while visuals convey the truth. Seeing a character shuffle awkwardly into a room could suggest they have something major to hide, or they're not as confident about an upcoming heist plan as their bragging may indicate.

Likewise, a character bursting into tears or a howl of laughter at the sight of a character dying says much more than clunky dialogue like "I hated that arrogant fool," or "He was my secret lover for the past six months!"

Excessive exposition separates the novice from the pro like nothing else. Great dialogue reveals a character's backstory with subtlety; poor lines declare it with all the sophistication of processed cheese in a can.

Audiences don't want to be spoon-fed. Subconsciously, everyone wants to work a little to figure out the narrative being played out on screen. Viewers like to piece together all the visual clues so as to feel smug and smart at the end of the day – *without* any of your characters stepping on their toes to let them know what they *should* be looking for.

Take this appalling example of bad exposition:

>   RAJ
>   Didn't your mom sleep with
>   everyone's dad and all your
>   middle school teachers? Isn't
>   that why you hate her?

The information contained in this exposition could be illustrated much more tastefully with visuals. Here's a way to *show* this part of the story rather than *telling* it:

```
INT. LIVING ROOM - NIGHT

John picks up the smashed photo frame and slides the photo of
his mother out from under the glass.

                                             FADE TO WHITE:

EXT. SCHOOL GATES - DAY - FLASHBACK

John's mother, TRACEY (32, short red dress, makeup), holds his
hand as they approach the school.

A DAD, bringing his daughter to school, spots Tracey and sends
her a seedy smile. Tracey avoids his stare.

                         TRACEY
            Have a nice day, honey — love you.

John witnesses the smile, reluctantly letting his mom kiss his
cheek. Tracey winces when she sees John can't even look at her.

                         TRACEY
                I said I love you.
A beat.
                          JOHN
                          Yep.

Tracey despondently watches John shuffle into the school.

                                             FADE TO WHITE:
```

```
INT. LIVING ROOM - NIGHT

Back with older John holding the photo of his mother. He wipes
a tear from his eye, then anger takes over as he scrunches up
the aging photo in a fist.
```

See how this emotional scene *showing* us the story of John's mother is so much better than Raj explaining it outright? *Show, don't tell.* Showing allows the audience to piece together the story themselves, which makes a far stronger impact. Without divulging the information directly via dialogue, we've learned about John's mother's appearance and his childhood confusion and shame.

Seeing John holding an old photo of his parent also suggests the two may not have spoken for a time. We wonder: is John still angry at his mother? Is he blaming himself for his lack of compassion? Or perhaps there's another reason.

While your script is of course meant to be filmed, firstly it must be read – so it's important to balance its dialogue and action. The rule of thumb is that in the final film edit, each page should last one minute on average. Dialogue is written down the center of the page with wide spacing, meaning a whole page of it takes less time to finish reading.

On the contrary, a page consisting of all stage direction takes longer to read. Strike the right balance between dialogue and stage direction to create a flowing screenplay that doesn't burn through the story too quickly or get drowned in detail.

Every genre has a different balance to strike. A comedy can be more propelled by dialogue – but you still have to combine spoken jokes with visual gags. No matter the genre, draw the audience in with curiosity. Fill your pages with intrigue instead of easy answers. Make them hungry for detail – but only feed them a crumb at a time.

Treat your dialogue like a sexy narrative striptease: all flirtation and quick peeks, building up to the show-stopping finale, in which you finally give the viewers what they've been waiting for.

Homework

Want to write dialogue to make Aaron Sorkin blush? Want to write dialogue to make Tarantino's weird backward cap blow off? (Seriously, what is that thing?) Just follow the exercises below.

Task 1
You wanna be a contender? You wanna be somebody?

When watching a movie, type up the dialogue being spoken on screen. This gets you in the habit of physically writing great professional dialogue, seeing it right in front of you; it embeds what dialogue should be into your mind and hands.

Task 2
Do I really sound like that?

Next time you're subtly observing people in your local coffee shop, note how they speak to each other. People don't speak in perfect sentences. Notice how people's speech is disjointed.

Notice how people communicate physically, too. Remember: you don't always need words. People give more away in their actions than their words.

This exercise will strengthen your ability to write authentic-sounding characters.

Next step

Jump in and write the first act of your script – the start of your "slab of clay" draft, what some writers call "draft zero". The point is to provide an overview or preview of your final product.

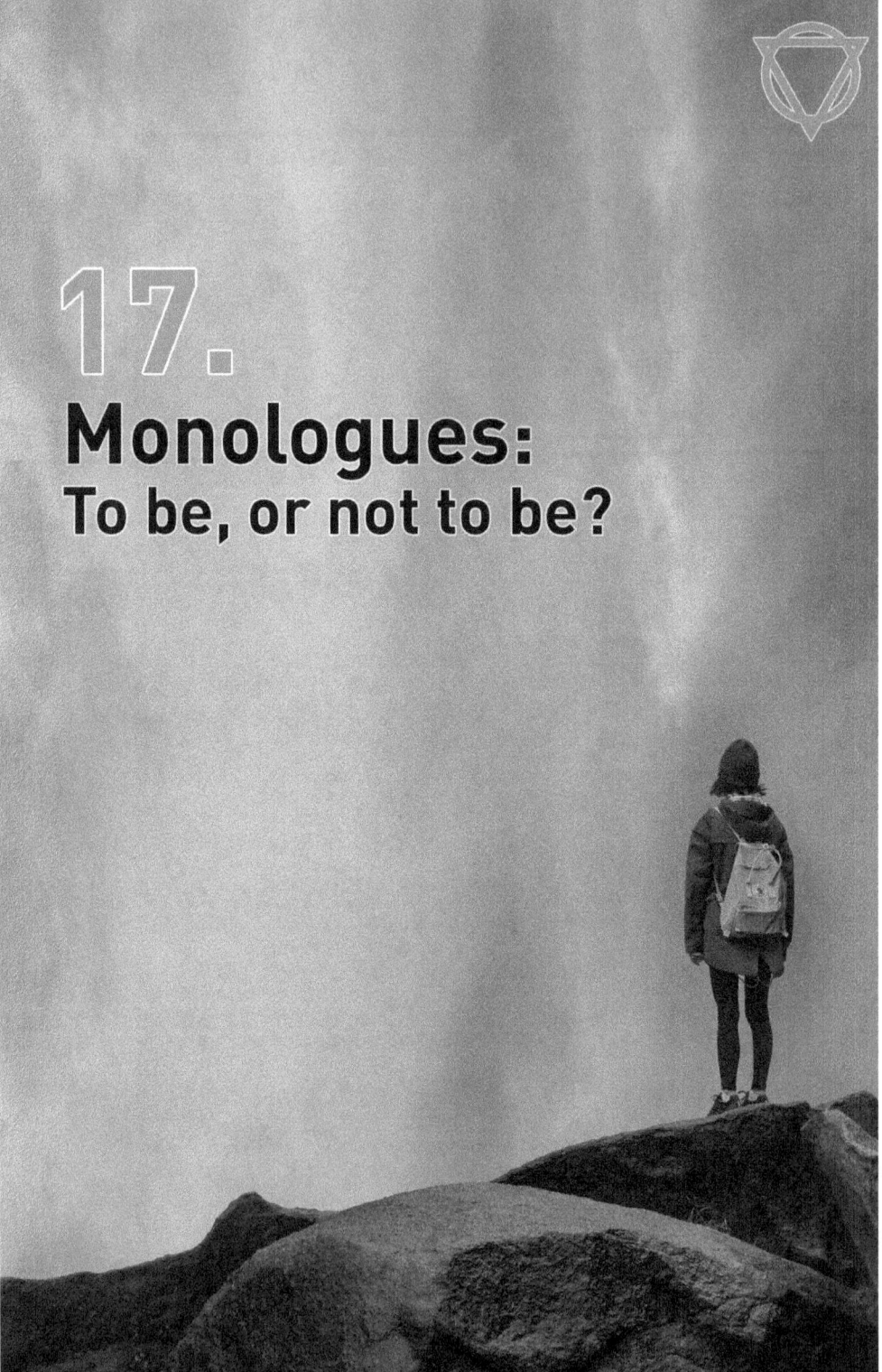

17.
Monologues:
To be, or not to be?

We should open this lesson with a bold, striking statement – something profound to shake you to your core and make you question your entire existence!

Instead, we're going to open with this: the monologue is a potent screenwriting technique. Done well, it packs a serious punch – which is why you must be careful with it. You don't want to knock out your audience!

Only use a monologue if it has a clear and tasteful purpose.

The monologue that opens *Black Panther*, for example, offers an explanation of the world of Wakanda and the motivations of the key characters, while also setting up the plot for the rest of the story. Each line is warranted and packs a punch of intrigue – those words have *earned* their place in the movie.

That's worth remembering if you feel compelled to drop a monologue of your own into your script. There's no room for excess – *every* word must be essential.

Monologues are like stories in miniature: they require a clear beginning, middle, and end.

There are two different types: *active* monologues and *narrative* monologues. When a character is trying to achieve something or take an action, that's an active monologue. Sometimes a character is desperate to change someone's mind or passionately argue his point of view.

Think of method madman Gary Oldman's rousing speech as Winston Churchill in *Darkest Hour*. The main objective of the British Bulldog's emotional declaration is to remind Parliament to continue fighting to the bitter end.

When a character is telling a story as an analogy to what's happening in the film or to explain the plot, it's a narrative monologue.

Towards the end of Luc Besson's *Valerian and the City of a Thousand Planets*, the victimized aliens explain their goal of reclaiming the animal that is key to their species's survival. The plot is explained within this monologue, but it also answers some of the mysteries littered throughout the movie.

A more sophisticated narrative monologue can be enjoyed in the opening of Guillermo del Toro's *The Shape of Water*. Giles reads a fairy tale about "a princess, the one she loved, and the monster who tried to tear them apart."

One of the best ways to learn how to write monologues is to study when *not* to use them. A monologue should never be used as a script hack for when you've run out of creative steam.

Saying in a four-page monologue what could have been expressed in a single phrase isn't just a cheap way to pad your script, it's also a fantastic way to waste your audience's time and insult their intelligence.

Don't have something purposeful or actionable to add to your script? Then don't use a monologue. But if your words are vital and rousing on every level, congratulations! You may just have a monologue that earns its place on the page.

Homework

We've warned you of the potential dangers of monologue writing – but you've been so inspired by monologues that you just *have* to write one.

We can never take... your freedom!
– Braveheart

Task 1

Pull those heartstrings!

Write an active monologue. Then, write a narrative monologue. They don't need to be about the idea you're working on; this is just an exercise.

Then find as many *different* possible ways to explain what has been explained in your monologue. This is good practice when you feel compelled to write a monologue; that way you'll have some ideas on top for other ways of conveying information in screenplays.

Task 2

Be the literary surgeon you were destined to be.

On YouTube, study the best monologues of all time. What is it specifically that makes you feel something, makes a statement, or aids the meaning of the story? Type your favorite monologue out.

Would this monologue still make sense if you removed any words? Now ask yourself the same question for the monologues you wrote in Task 1.

Next step

Feeling the pressure? Got some itchy fingers? It's time to jump in and write the first half of the second act (Act 2A) of your movie. You can do it – we're rooting for you!

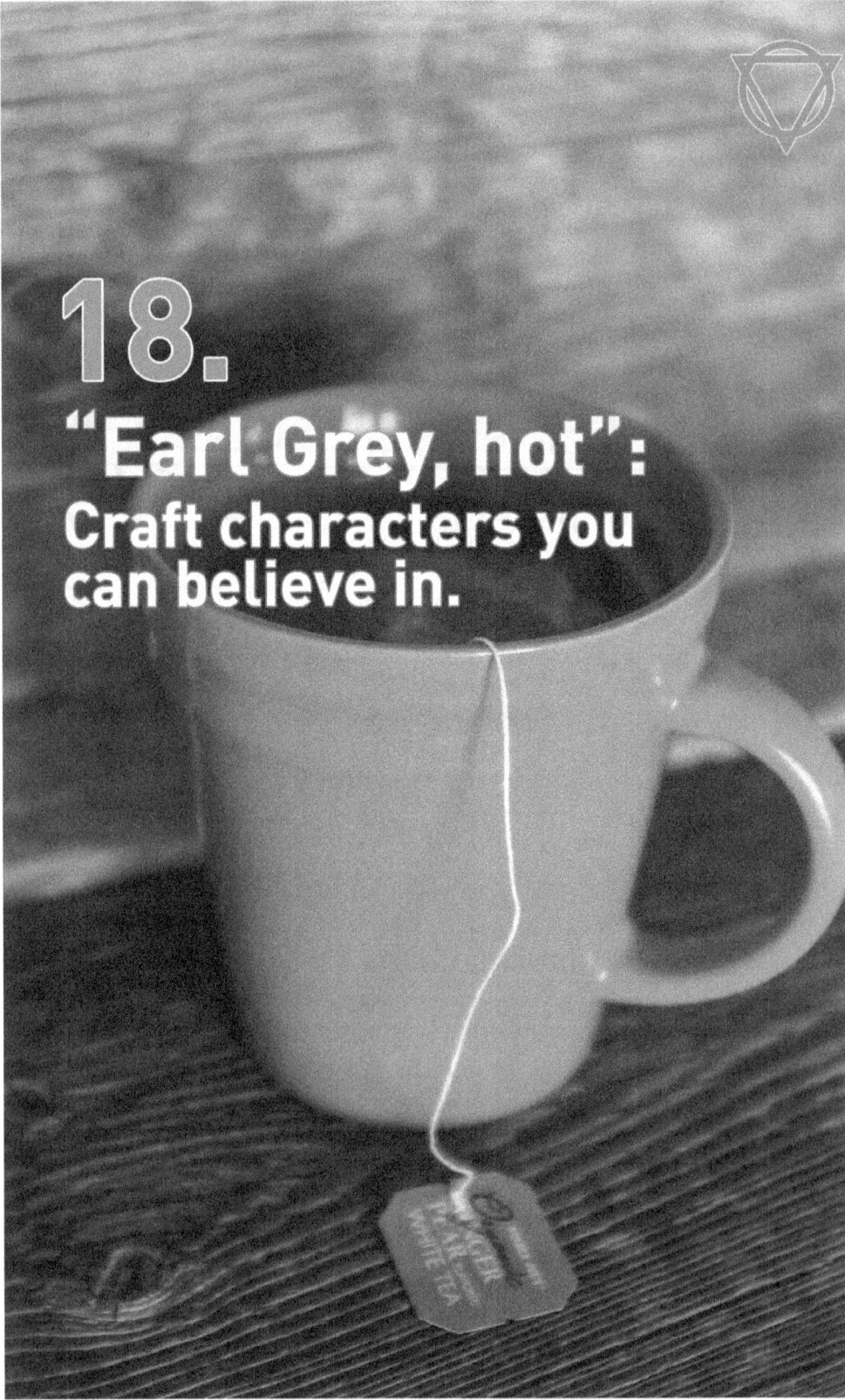

Here's something to put in neon right above your workstation: "Characters are a metaphor for human nature."

That's a quote from screenwriting expert Robert McKee – and it's true. This is why it's so important you take the time to develop characters with *real* depth.

Stories hinge around how their characters choose to act under pressure. The stronger the pressure applied to the character, the more satisfying his eventual achievement will be.

RuPaul closes every episode of *Drag Race* by musing, "If you can't love yourself, how in the hell you gon' love anybody else?" The same can be asked about your characters: if you don't believe in them, how the hell do you expect your audience to?

You've seen more than one film with humdrum, one-dimensional characters. Why is that so important to note? Because dimensions take form as contradictions, and when we see them in human nature they're utterly captivating.

When we're introduced to *Westworld*'s Dolores Abernathy, she's little more than a damsel in distress who could never hurt a sentient being. But as the story progresses, so does Dolores.

We learn there's more to her than just a pre-programmed robot – she's smart & strong. Most notably, we discover she's more than capable of murder. This adds a compelling mystery to the character.

The reverse is the case in *Blade Runner 2049*. Special Agent K is a replicant, or android, tasked with hunting down his own kind. Our interest and curiosity are piqued when the depth of the character's emotions is revealed; he's no cold killing machine after all.

The protagonist must be the most multi-faceted character of your script, in order to ensure maximum empathy. Want to craft great characters worth believing in? As RuPaul would again say: "You better work!"

Crafting multidimensional characters takes time and effort. To help you craft yours, this lesson's homework features a big list of questions to ask when defining your core characters. Some questions might come across as banal, but the point is to get you intimately familiar with how the character looks, sounds, behaves – maybe even smells.

Understanding your characters – even something as everyday as the beer they choose or which underwear they favor and why – will help you immerse yourself in the complexity of their identities.

A character must be a living, breathing human (or android) you can believe in and, most importantly, *empathize* with – flaws, failures, farts, and all. She'll be your representative in your fictional universe, so you want her to feel real enough to guide you through it.

Your objective is to make the audience willingly suspend their disbelief and put themselves in this person's shoes. If your character doesn't come across as real, your audience won't give a flying fruit roll-up what happens to her.

When an audience cares about a character, they're *invested* in her. They imagine how they would react in whichever situation the character has found herself. Make your character seem alive in your head, and she'll come to life on the page – and the screen, too.

Want some inspiration? Think of all the people who have ever made a deep impact on you, or are at least memorable for some reason. Write down everything about them that is remarkable. Make a list of their good, and bad, traits.

Used to help inform the development of a character, this list could be just what you need to help build a multidimensional character, as it comes from a real person.

The next step is to create a character biography. This can be as long or as short as you'd like, but it's important for you to figure out exactly where your characters have been up to this point in the story, so they feel as real as possible.

Write your script as though your characters have a life *outside* your tale. If you do that well, the characters will live within the imagination and hearts of your audience too.

Homework

If you've paid any attention to this lesson, you know the importance of characters' richness and depth. Clear some space in your day, 'cause the homework for this lesson is . . . shall we say, comprehensive. When it comes to character, there's no such thing as too much detail.

1. First and last names
2. Precise age
3. Height
4. Hair color / straight or curly / long or short / stylish or ordinary

5. Always go to same barber, or cut it him/herself?
6. Middle name – embarrassed about it? Does it mean something?
7. Eye color
8. Foot size
9. Fat, thin or in-between? How so?
10. Confident looking in the mirror?
11. Care about his/her looks?
12. Secret physical thing proud of & ashamed of
13. Slob or tidy?
14. Clothing fashion/style? Common clothing color(s)?
15. Hat?
16. Footwear
17. Hand description
18. Personal hygiene
19. Parents alive?
20. Mother's maiden name
21. Mother's & father's occupations
22. Social class
23. Wealth level & changes over lifetime & family's before birth
24. Happy or unhappy childhood?
25. Favorite childhood toy
26. Birthplace, childhood location
27. Own room, or share?
28. Childhood bedroom wall decorations
29. Favorite place in the childhood home
30. Backyard, frontyard? Describe.
31. Any pets? Pet deaths?
32. Favorite childhood/comfort food
33. Successful at school academically, or struggle?
34. Single-sex school or mixed?
35. Mainly female or male friends?
36. Any siblings? What ages? How were the relationships?
37. Parents' favorite sibling
38. Prefer one parent to the other?
39. Family: calm or lively? Creative?
40. Strict parents?
41. Suffered any abuse?
42. Attractive as a teenager?
43. Popular at school?
44. Best / worst subject?
45. Name of best friend
46. Age when met this friend?
47. Still friends?
48. First kiss: first & last name
49. Age at first kiss
50. Still know first kiss partner?
51. Age when virginity lost? Great / comic / letdown?
52. Age left parents' home, destination
53. Any higher education?
54. Close to family as an adult?
55. Changed much since childhood?
56. Feelings about sex now
57. Political leanings
58. Capital punishment pro/con?
59. Vote history
60. Favorite books

61. Passions / hobbies
62. First album purchased
63. Social media use
64. First job
65. Spiritual beliefs & practices
66. Fears & phobias
67. Residential location & type
68. Own/rent?
69. Kitchen appearance
70. Culinary skills
71. Typical breakfast
72. Favorite food
73. Favorite drink (hot/cold)
74. 5 things in fridge
75. Morning or evening person?
76. Fitness level & activities
77. Health? Diseases? Disabilities?
78. Medications
79. Sleep quality / amount
80. Favorite films & TV shows
81. Heroes
82. Typical evening activities
83. Own a car? Bike? Other vehicles?
84. Bed sheet color
85. 3 adjectives a typical stranger would use to describe (first impression)
86. Areas lacking talent / skill
87. Desires for skills not possessed
88. Cunning or honest?
89. Situations for dishonesty
90. Punctuality / lateness
91. Concern level of others' opinions (of character)
92. Diligence / laziness
93. What would this person's recurring dream be about?
94. Travelled widely? Where? With family, friends, or alone?
95. Travel goals
96. Diet – vegetarian etc.
97. Alcohol, drug use?
98. Phone screensaver
99. Children / grandchildren / want children?
100. Romantic relationships: history, present
101. Romantic desires / goals / attitudes
102. Countryside or the city?
103. Worst failure
104. Greatest strength not aware of
105. Attitude toward money
106. Bank account? Amounts?
107. Other material wealth
108. Tend to live in the present, past, future?
109. Introvert or extrovert?
110. Sense of humor
111. Leader or follower?
112. Typical behavior at parties
113. Current friends
114. Sports? Play/watch? Competitive?
115. Musical aptitude: sing, play instrument?
116. Ambitious? How so?
117. Traits admired in others
118. Seasickness?

119. Worst habit
120. Quirky habits
121. Tan / pale / dark etc?
122. Attitude towards death
123. Ideal age of death
124. Shames
125. Attitude towards medicine, alternative medicine
126. Mismatch between self-perception & reality (intelligence, charm, ability, etc.)
127. Pajama description
128. Bath or shower?
129. Perfume / cologne / aftershave
130. Others' behavior that triggers offense to be taken
131. Favorite charities?
132. Swimming ability
133. Wishes to be someone else?
134. Most embarrassing situation ever
135. Guilty pleasure song
136. Feel he/she deserves to be happy?
137. What causes him/her to feel vulnerable
138. What would you say to this character right now to make them believe in his/her future?

Who is your protagonist?

Open your trusty notebook or note-taking software and delineate the following about your main character:

Next step

Still awake? Then it's time to get writing. Own the second half of act two (Act 2B)!

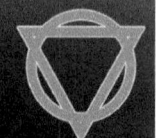

19.
Tears for days:
How to make the audience care

What is it that makes us latch onto characters? What inclines us to care so much we might even write fanfiction about them? Not that we ever would do that... *ahem.*

Just because you've thought of an interesting main character doesn't mean audiences will give a damn if they live or die. You might think adorning your character with interesting traits and making them seem as real as possible would be enough to make an audience care, but that just isn't always so.

Making a character audiences actually care about comes back to the Hero's Journey. You'll need all the dynamite notes you made during that lesson to help the final crafting of your main character.

You've given your protagonist a goal to pursue, and therefore know her need will overlap with her want. Make sure your goal is specifically designed to deal with her flaw, and audiences will root for your character until the bitter end, because they'll be able to identify with her goal.

Audience members also identify with the choices a character makes in pursuit of his goal. That's because choices illuminate certain aspects of a character. His flaws and ultimate goal are what make us care about him – so it's essential to make them interesting.

We care about Mildred in Three Billboards Outside Ebbing, Missouri because her flaws are so interesting and understandable. As she antagonizes the police about solving her murdered daughter's case, we see she's socially inept, violent, and hilarious – but she's also a mother in mourning.

Mildred can be shocking and volatile in her pursuit for justice, but she also has a goal with which we can empathize. Her contradictions make us want to witness her journey; we're invested in its outcome.

This is the kind of dynamic that screams greatness. Mildred is hellbent on revenge and her many flaws are evident from the get-go. Her capricious nature is at odds with her goal; to achieve it, she must learn to work with others.

Remember: actions speak louder than words. You can't rely solely on dialogue to make an audience care. Actions show us who the character really is; words are merely confetti.

In our next lesson, you'll learn about why that's the case, as we delve into crafting the ultimate "big bad" for your story.

Homework

The homework for this lesson requires you to notice characters' decision-making. Watch and learn how the screenwriting maestros make you empathize and latch onto their carefully crafted characters – whether you want to or not. Thought you had a choice, didn't you!

Character judgement day

Take a notepad and pen for the next film you watch and note down every time the protagonist makes a decision in the story. When the film is over look at the list of decisions.

The list is proof of an active protagonist who drives the story and makes us empathize with them. Every time the character makes a decision, we ask ourselves what decision we would personally make in his or her shoes.

The character must keep making decisions in order to keep us on board with the story. Make sure you do the same for your protagonist.

Next step

Whip the third act of your movie into shape. This might take you a few days, so we'll go gentle on you!

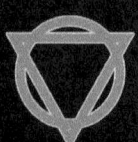

20.
The bigger the baddie, the bolder the victory

We'll let you in on a little secret: the worse your antagonist, the better your film.

That might be something you already know, but one of the most important hooks to hang your script off is the biggest, baddest villain you can muster.

Look at Strickland in *The Shape of Water*. The guy is a fearless, sociopathic brute who will stop at nothing to please his superiors, stroke his own ego, and punish the Amphibian Man.

He's an authority figure with the power to thwart Elisa's goal of protecting the creature, and he isn't afraid to play dirty. After all, this guy washes his hands *before* he goes to the bathroom. Ugh!

This type of villain ensures maximum tension, suspense, and devastation for the protagonist. He's the type of big bad that works wonders setting up high stakes – the harder it is to overcome the antagonist, the more riveting the story.

If the villain is easy to overcome, your plot loses its stakes; the story won't be exciting, nor will it have longevity.

Remember: an antagonist doesn't have to be a person. Antagonism refers to any force preventing the lead character from achieving his goal. It is the *something* or *someone* standing in his way.

Your villain is what makes your hero stand out and dazzle. Whatever shape your antagonist takes, you want it to be crafted just as well as the protagonist is.

Some of the best antagonists ever seen on screen have been carefully humanized. Think of the Armitage family in *Get Out*, whose excessively polite nature humanizes them in the lead-up to the reveal of their insidious true intentions, making their betrayal all the more harrowing.

In *Big Little Lies*, Perry Wright appears to be a doting family man, but is slowly revealed to be an abusive rapist. In the middle of the story we even root for him to change in response to catching a glimpse of goodness in him.

Realize that, if you look through the eyes of your villain, she is the hero in her story and the protagonist is the villain. So give her the same treatment as your protagonist.

The villain needs a backstory and biography so you know exactly where she's been and what she's been doing prior to your story. In her first few scenes, it's important to humanize her somehow.

Good and evil aren't always the polar opposites fairy tales had you believe as a child. Look at Betty Cooper in *Riverdale*: a character who can flip between good and bad by changing wigs! As Betty herself would state: As human beings, it's our nature that we all have darkness in us – and goodness as well.

No one is *purely* evil – not even a killing machine like *Friday the 13th's* Jason Voorhees. He even built a shrine to his dead mother with her decapitated head as a centerpiece, proving he's actually a low-key momma's boy.

If Jason can have a bit of goodness to him, so can your antagonist. Subtle humanization of your villain makes your audience empathize.

Some scripts use this technique so that one empathizes with the antagonist to the point of momentarily coming around to his way of thinking – making his defeat all the more emotional.

Erik in *Black Panther* is a character abandoned in a poverty-stricken neighborhood who becomes involved in gang culture and is further brutalized by service in the military. The character's screwiness is completely understandable; we empathize with his treatment and why he's so determined to return to Wakanda and rule.

The only things that ensure Erik remains an antagonist are how he achieves his goal, and we continue to see his emotional side when he has a vision of his dead father.

Erik is a multidimensional villain who almost outshines the hero: the sign of a great antagonist. You'll find films and TV shows are often remembered for their antagonists rather than their heroes – so craft yours carefully and with humanity.

Homework

Time to start piecing together your villains. Gollum, Loki, Hans Gruber, Hannibal Lecter, and Norman Bates all paved the way for sympathetic villains you just love to hate. Add yours to that list!

I do wish we could chat for longer, but I'm having an old friend for dinner.
– Hannibal Lecter

Come up with a few bad guys. Make them different and as bad as you possibly can. They should be multi-dimensional and humanized.

Develop a strong sense of belief in your antagonists. Remember, inside the mind of the antagonists, *they* are the heroes. Pay as much attention to the antagonist in your film as you do the protagonist.

Now you have a greater understanding of who your protagonist and antagonist are, go back to your script and start enriching the characters.

Next step

Keep on truckin' with act three!

21.
Enter late – get out early.

Houston, we have a problem! See if you can diagnose the problems with this awful scene:

```
INT. STEVE'S HOUSE — NIGHT

Steve opens the front door, locks it, and throws his keys in a
small metal tray. He unties his shoelaces, removes his shoes,
and proceeds to the living room.

Steve proceeds to walk into the sitting room, slumps down onto
the sofa, and slings his bag on the floor.

He stretches to pick up the remote but instead finds a note.

It reads: "If you're reading this, I'm dead".

Steve processes this information.

                        STEVE
            What? But why would she . . . oh god!
            Oh god, I've got to stop her!
```

Did you catch the issue? Surely not all this scene is actually necessary.

Less is more. Give the reader the maximum amount of information with the fewest words possible.

Treat it like an awful party at your ex's house: you want to enter late and leave as early as possible. Dive into each scene as late as possible and leave it as early as you can. *This* is what makes screenplays flow by maintaining a suspenseful pace.

A common sign of starting a scene too early is pointless dialogue. Your characters don't need to greet each other unless it's integral to the scene – nor do we need to see them leave.

If you've seen *The Room*, you'll know why the line "Oh, hi Mark" has become an iconic phrase: it's *definitely* not because it's a sparkling piece of dialogue that flows well. As Alfred Hitchcock famously said, "A screenplay is someone's life with all the boring bits cut out."

Returning to our awful script: no one cares about Steve locking the door, putting his keys in the tray, or untying his shoes, because it's unlikely these actions are vitally important to the story. Instead, the scene could start with Steve jumping on the sofa, tossing his bag aside, and reaching for the controller but finding the note instead.

We also shouldn't have to suffer Steve gradually processing the information and delivering a frantic response. How about a smash cut to Steve frantically trying to phone the woman who left him the note and leaving a series of desperate voicemails?

Seeing Steve's actions in response to the note is far more interesting than *hearing* his immediate reaction via dialogue. Cutting straight to it is riveting and keeps the pace of your script pounding.

It's the golden rule that'll keep your screenplay tighter than Terry Cruz's abs: *Get in late and leave early.*

Cut as much as you can out of the beginning and end of each scene and see if it still works. As soon as the goal of each scene is achieved, get out of there!

Homework

This particular assignment might just be one of the most useful craft exercises you can do. If you keep practising this style of writing long after you're done with this course, every single script of yours will be a page-turner. So don't skip this homework!

To cut a long story short . . .

Think of a crazily interesting event that has either happened to you, or someone else. Write it like a movie, following the rules in the lesson: cut all the boring stuff out. Get in late on your scenes and leave early, and you'll be practising your craft like a pro.

Next step

Show the third act who's boss, and finish it. Go back through your whole script and trim down each scene, with particular focus on each one's start and end.

22.
Bourne again:
Infuse your characters with purpose & motivation.

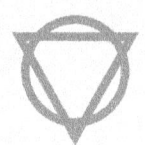

You've crafted multidimensional characters who feel real & relatable, and you've given them a journey worth caring about. What's next? You want to infuse those suckers with some serious motivation!

A character's motivation is something to which viewers try to relate. They want to understand fully why characters do what they do.

Numerous excellent examples can be found in season one of *Westworld*, in which all the main characters are absolutely hellbent on achieving their goals. Maeve wants to escape the park after realizing her sadistic purpose. Young William wants to protect Dolores because he believes she is conscious and also *hopelessly* in love with him. Meanwhile, Dolores is determined to discover her true identity & purpose.

These are solid, totally understandable motivations that make the actions of the characters more credible to the audience; having realistic motivations anchors your story with a relatable resonance.

Dolores Abernathy is actually a prime example of how purpose & motivation interact to form the architecture of *Westworld*'s plot. Her purpose is to become the benchmark for the evolution of the hosts – which incidentally sets up the the show's second season. Dolores's purpose is what anchors its entire plot in place. By the end of season one, she is reborn and takes control of her own story.

We might not be robots like the hosts of *Westworld*, but they're presented as sentient beings whose purpose is mostly to be abused by humans. We subconsciously place ourselves in their shoes and realize we'd probably go medieval on the sadistic guests too.

Strong motivation creates deep tension – it's a great way of upping the stakes of your story. Basic techniques to up the ante for your characters include survival, protection of children, finding shelter, ordering a White Castle feast before closing time, and the biggest stakes of all: life & death.

A better way of understanding the different kinds of motivations your character could have is by studying Maslow's hierarchy of needs:

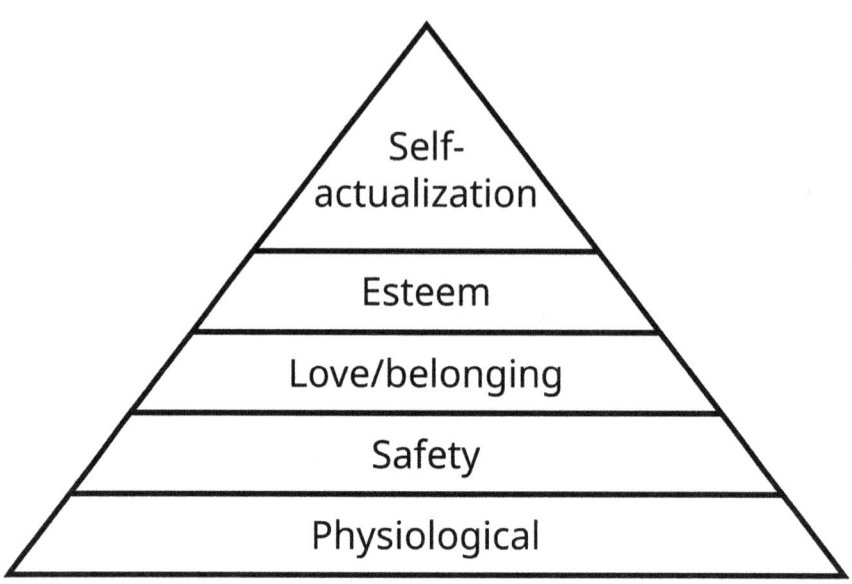

At the lowest level, physiological motivations include basic survival needs like shelter, food, and water. Next come safety motivations: not just protecting oneself from physical threats, but also employment, making rent, paying bills, and general health.

At the middle of the motivational hierarchy are love and belonging: friendships, romantic connections, and family. After that is esteem, which relates to your character's social status, freedom, and general self-confidence.

At the top of it all lies self-actualization, the desire to achieve your full potential: a sort of enlightened state of total well-being.

Maslow's pyramid is a killer tool for delving into your characters' motivations. Where in that pyramid do your protagonist's motivations lie? Are they rudimentary, just trying to stay safe? Desperate for love? Looking to feel confident and capable, or rising through social rankings?

Understanding your characters' incentives on such a deep level not only allows your audience to connect with them, but also helps your story flow with purpose. That's something we'll be examining further in our next lesson, as we investigate writing seamlessly flowing scenes.

Homework

Film theory like this is often overlooked, and stories suffer for it. Fish for nuggets of truth like these in everything you watch. This kind of understanding will make you a screenwriting supergenius!

There's no place like home

In some TV shows or movies, pinpoint exactly where on Maslow's hierarchy the protagonist's motivations reside. Pick films & shows vastly different from each other to provide a varying outlook on story.

Make a firm decision on where the protagonist in your script will fall on the hierarchy.

Next step

Page count too high? Go through your script and see if any dialogue can be removed.

Remember: actions speak louder than words.

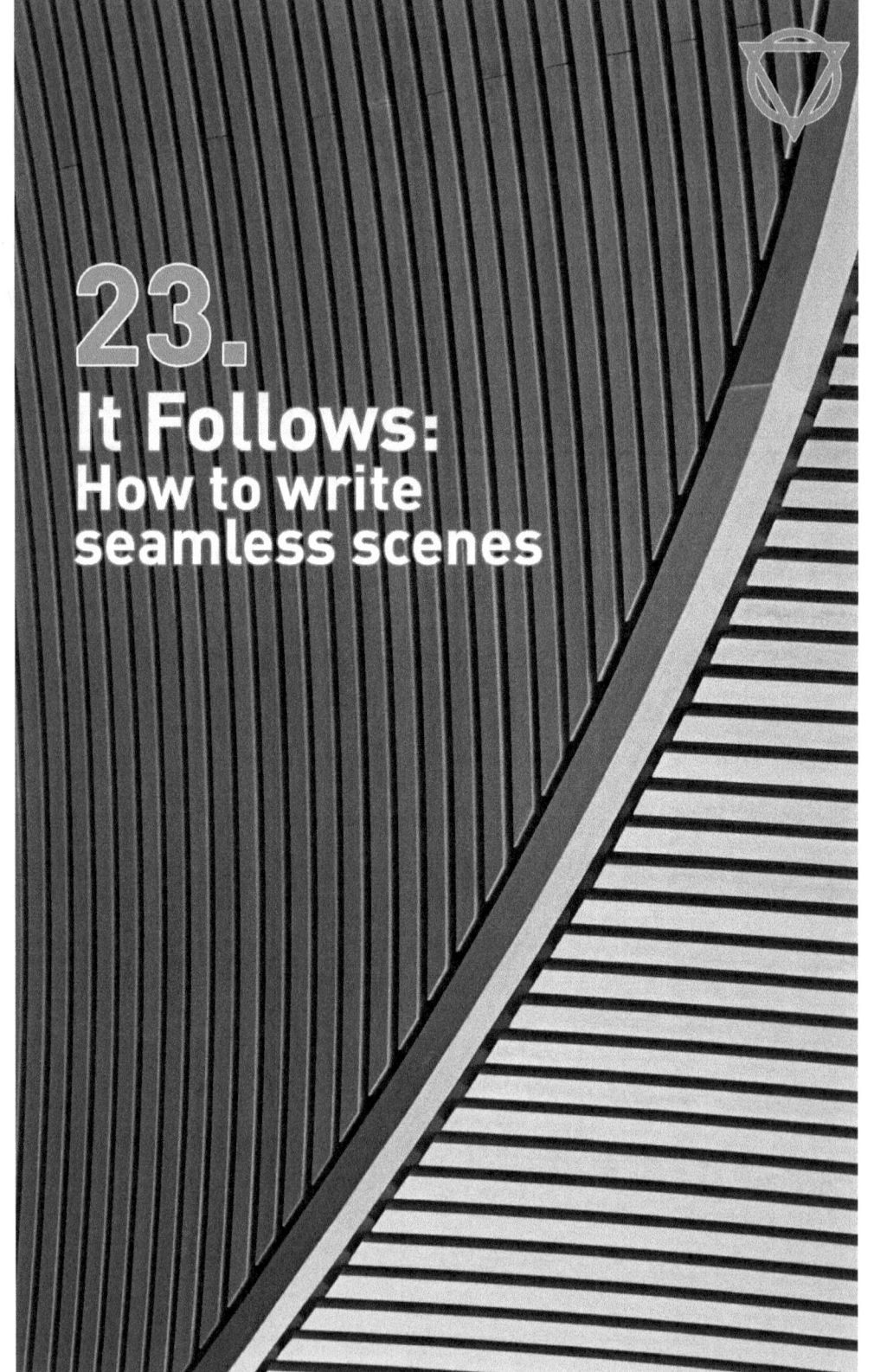

23.
It Follows:
How to write seamless scenes

Ever wondered if there's more to the magic of storytelling? You know there's something enchanting about the way a particular movie or TV show moves forward, but you're not exactly sure *why*. What is it that makes it flow so well?

We already touched on that in "Enter late, leave early", which is how we know you're ready for the next step: crafting beautifully flowing scenes. Once you can construct seamless scenes, it will distinguish you as an experienced writer who knows how to spin words into pure gold.

For this educational trip, we're going to be taking a journey to *Riverdale*. We'll examine the scenes of a single episode of The CW hit teen series to break down exactly how each scene flows so well into the next.

This episode is "Chapter Two: Touch of Evil", predominantly an Archie-led story. As well as involving various shots of KJ Apa taking his top off and looking puzzled, it also features the following scenes:

1. Jughead introduces the episode with an opening *film noir*-style monologue.
2. Archie attempts to placate some guilt by begging Betty to talk to him. He's unsuccessful.
3. Archie sneaks over to Miss Grundy's house. He expresses his desire to come clean to the police regarding what they know about Jason Blossom's death, even if that means exposing the illegal relationship between Archie and Miss Grundy.
4. Archie's dad asks why Archie snuck out. Is there something on his mind?
5. Betty's mom tells her not to spend time with Archie anymore.
6. Betty *immediately* spends time with Archie by walking to school with him.
7. Archie broods over his Jason Blossom guilt while in school.
8. Betty & Kevin talk about Archie and how hunky he looks now.
9. Veronica apologizes to Betty for kissing Archie.
10. Sheriff Keller announces Jason's death is being treated as a homicide and urges anyone who knows something to come forward.
11. Archie doesn't come forward, but does stare at a photo of Jason while looking very guilty.
12. Jughead quizzes Archie about where he was on the day of Jason's death.

Did you notice how the beats tend to flow so smoothly from one to the next? Every scene moves the plot forward.

The first ten minutes are focused on Archie's guilt and the increasing pressure around him to *do the right thing*. Everywhere he turns, he faces a different form of conflict and all of it is connected to the one question: will Archie risk everything to come forward and share what he knows about Jason's death?

The scenes flow because the key scenes relate to one character and his clear predicament. The charming subplot about Betty doesn't distract, but serves to lighten the episode's otherwise tense tone.

Very effective visual imagery helps connect scenes further. While discussing Jason and the investigation with Archie, Cheryl plunges a scalpel into a dead animal in biology class. We then immediately cut to Jason's corpse on an autopsy table.

But it isn't just beautiful teenagers, murderous intrigue, and cute segues helping it flow. This particular episode of *Riverdale* also excels at finishing so many scenes on a question – a technique that captivates the audience to remain glued to their seats, eager for what comes next.

Leaving a scene on an unanswered question will give you the perfect balance of intrigue and satisfaction. However, you can't just tease the audience without offering up some juicy details. Like Archie's suggestive habit of removing his tee at any given moment, you have to give the audience a little, and make them wonder a lot.

This can't be done with every scene, but it certainly ought to be done with most. Here's how *Riverdale* ends some scenes of this episode by posing big questions:

1. **Jughead catches Archie and Miss Grundy behaving suspiciously frisky together at school.**
What will Jughead do with this knowledge? Will he update his blog? Will he tell the principal?

2. **Archie's dad knows something is going on with his son and persuades him to come clean, whatever it may be.**
Will Archie do what his dad suggests? If so, how will he do that and who will he tell? What consequences could telling the truth have on everyone?

3. Cheryl unexpectedly flees from her big cheerleading show in front of everyone. Veronica finds her sobbing, and Cheryl weeps that Jason was supposed to come back.
Is this a huge twist? Are the undead about to walk through *Riverdale*? Was Jason's death part of a nefarious plan gone wrong? And what exactly does Cheryl know that she hasn't told the cops?

Many of the questions left unanswered in scenes like these are answered later. Consider structuring each scene the same way you do a story: give it a beginning, a middle, and an end with a question or a cliffhanger as a closer. The next scene that picks up that plotline can then start with its resolution. When used in sequential scenes, the natural consequence of this technique is – you guessed it – scenes that flow well from one to the next.

The easiest places to spot this technique are at episode endings and prior to commercial breaks. The juicy scenes just before the ads run often feature burning questions so as to ensure you stick around for the answer, and the final scene has the biggest question because it needs to burn in your mind for the next week.

The massive hook at the end of this *Riverdale* episode features an unexpected twist: just as Archie plucks up the courage to confess to the principal what he knows about Jason, the police are already at school – except they're not here for him. They're here for Cheryl, who appears to know exactly why.

A series of mysteries float in this scene's wake. Why are the police interested in Cheryl? How is she involved in Jason's death and what does she know? Will Archie still talk to the principal in light of this development? This single huge hook raises at least four pivotal questions.

Hooks are an essential part of story design – without them, the thrust of your story comes off weak and uninteresting. If you want to keep your audience hooked, write sharp, seamless scenes brimming with questions and your plot will be irresistible to all.

Homework

Want to captivate the audience by the guts and keep them hooked into your story like helpless fish? Just execute the hidden gems in this homework and you'll be flying high.

Be a weaver – like a beaver.

Notepad and pen time again! Yes, you need to watch some more TV & films for this one.

Actively watch your show/movie and keep a keen eye on how the scenes transition from one to another.

- Do they flow between each other with visuals?
- Does the scene end on a question which is answered in the next scene?
- How does the scene arrangement keep you captivated as a viewer?

Next step

Do your scenes end on a question? Go back through your script and make sure they do.

24.
Who likes short shorts?

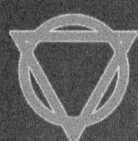

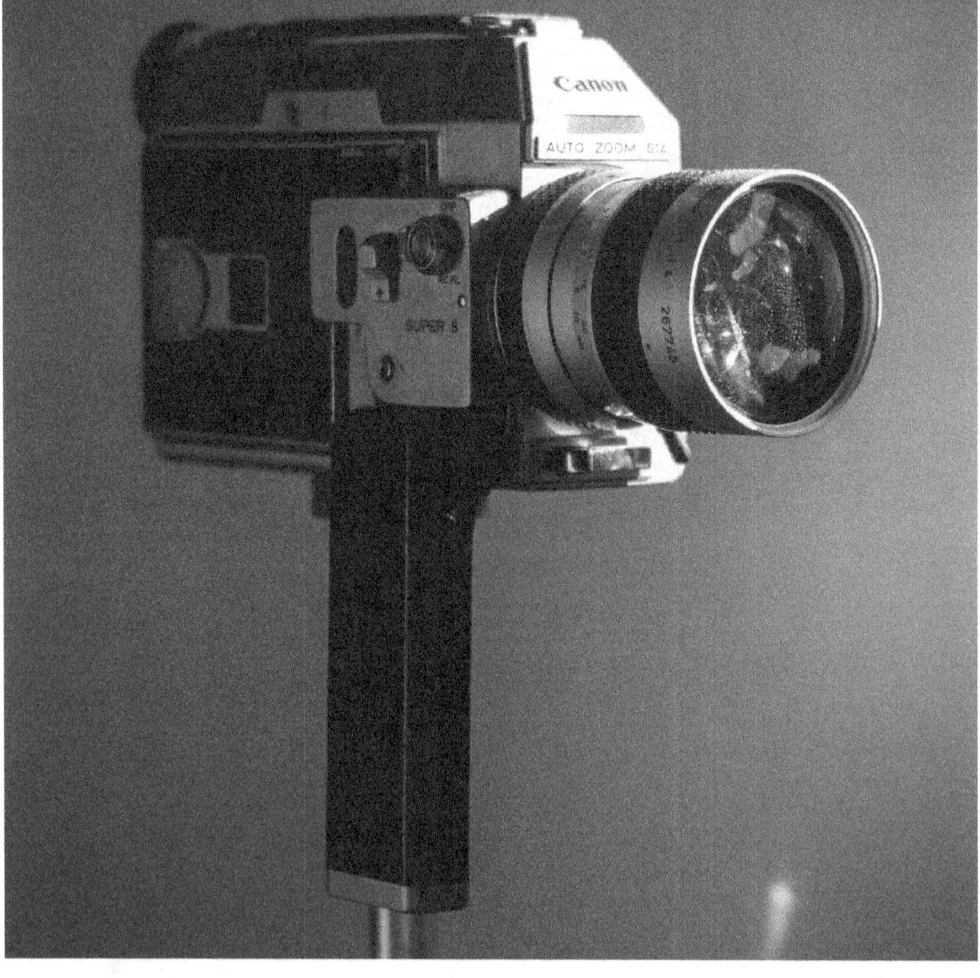

What is a short film and what does it take to write a good one? Let's begin by defining the different types of short film.

There's the microshort, which lasts approximately as long as a teenage lovemaking session at around two or three minutes. The medium short, the most common, comes in around five to fifteen minutes. And the BAFTA short – which is how you impress the British – has an average length of twenty to thirty minutes.

Then there's the Oscar short – which is how you become chummy with Timothée Chalamet at an Academy Awards afterparty – which features an average running time of forty minutes or less.

We know the prospect of writing a short film only two minutes long may not be hugely exciting – but we do urge you to consider it. A 90-second movie can help draw attention to your talents. If a film can prompt big emotions, unique thoughts, or bust a gut with laughter in such a short duration, it will definitely be memorable.

As you take in all the wisdom in this course so far and apply it to a script, there's a chance you might not be able to utilize every new skill. This is the beauty of the short film: you can try out different ideas and refine your writing skills. It's an achievable format, the perfect size for experimentation.

Short films offer an opportunity for practice. Working on a few different ideas will likely lead to a satisfying finale: the day you finally develop that bodacious script you're proud as a peacock to enter into every film festival possible.

We're also cuckoo for short films because they're the favored format for independent film festivals. These can only screen so many films and therefore tend to opt for shorts as opposed to features. Festival programmers would much rather show a couple dozen five-minute shorts than one 120-minute feature.

If you keep your script as tight and short as possible, that will drastically increase the number of festivals for which your film will be eligible. The more festivals your film enters, the more people you can wow – and the closer you'll be to that Oscar party where Greta Gerwig challenges you to a dance-off.

It isn't easy to write a condensed story. But that's also what a makes good short films stand out. The hard work will be evident, so be as patient and diligent as you can while writing.

Bear in mind the average attention span lasts about ten minutes. After that, we start drifting off and daydreaming about what we'll make for dinner, and whether

Jennifer Lawrence likes burritos. Use that fact to your advantage and get to your ending before your reader's mind starts to wander.

Most screenwriters struggle to keep the length of their scripts down – and in all likelihood so will you. Here are a couple of tips that will help you along:

Firstly, hit the ground running. Treat the pages as though you're carving into solid gold on which you can't waste words. Remember the lesson about getting in late and leaving early? One of its biggest boons is keeping your story concise.

You need to hook your audience within the first few seconds of your script. Start your story as if you're dropping in on the character precisely at that pivotal moment right before her life takes a sharp turn.

The other important tip: stick to one idea. Beginning writers often try to say far too much in too short a span of time. We're sure you have a lot to say about this crazy world of ours.

But don't cram *all* those feelings, ideas, and observations into your script. Break up your ideas into short films that provide you the space to explore each idea separately. Ignore this tip, and your story could become convoluted & cumbersome when it should be slick & lean.

Writing a phenomenal short film requires discipline and restraint, but also the guts to believe you have the talent required. Dig deep and discover your swagger; work hard and with grit; write concisely, but think big.

You have numerous short scripts within you just waiting to be perfected. One of them could be the ten-minute movie that enraptures the world.

Homework

The best way to learn how the limits of short film can be pushed and experimented with is simply by watching the best of the best. These guys are up-and-coming talents on the top of their game, so take note.

We like short shorts!

Get yourself on Vimeo and watch as many short films as you possibly can. Find award-winning shorts if you can – see what you're up against.

Watch many different types of shorts too. See what can be achieved in a 90-second story. If you can find them, the Oscars shorts will offer inspiration.

Next step

Go back to your opening scenes. Brainstorm all the alternative ideas that could hurl your story into motion faster. Take the most cogent ideas, and update your script.

25.
Be a writer – not a director.

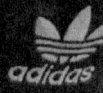

Writing camera angles and shots in your script is a screenwriting sin. Do it and you'll stall the pace of your script and make yourself an enemy to the director.

If you're using your script as a calling card for collaboration, then it's even more important. If your script is stuffed with actions for the director, it's unlikely they'll be interested. Remember, the final product will be an equal collaboration. Once you finish the screenplay, it's the director who begins to tell the story.

Instead of making yourself look amateurish by inserting camera angles or shot suggestions on every page, trust the director to know exactly where to put the camera. As a screenwriter, your opinions on direction will likely hold little influence to the final cut anyways. Keep those ideas off the page and just concentrate on being a dynamite wordsmith.

Imagine how you'd feel if the director gave *you* notes on how you should rewrite the script: you're halfway through shooting and she tells you she wants your gutsy heroine to throw on a nice dress and get married instead of pulling out the big guns and destroying the monster. Telling a director how to direct works the same way.

A screenplay gives the reader the smallest amount of information to understand what's happening. By adding specific directions, you're adding clutter that takes the reader out of your story. Instead of brimming with emotion, humor, horror, or tension, your story will instead feel clinical.

You want your script to be read for the story, period. Don't let anything get in the way of that.

Homework

We know you're a visionary genius and your script is a work of art that must be filmed exactly how you imagined it. But that's just not the way production works, buddy!

That's my job!

Read through your script and see if you've accidentally directed the story anywhere. If so, direct *yourself* to delete those actions.

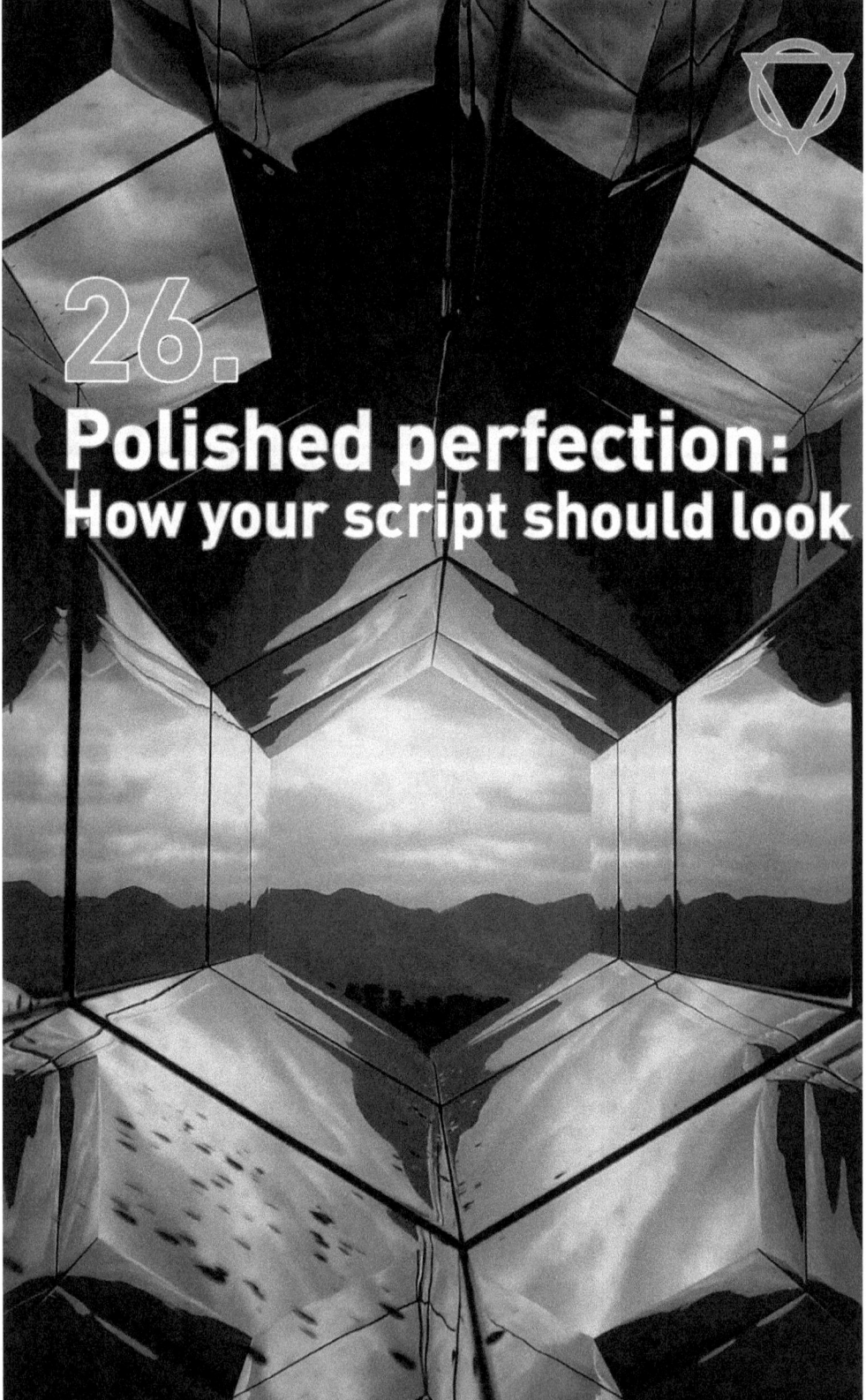

26.
Polished perfection:
How your script should look

You now have everything ready to smash out your masterpiece. It's officially time to type up your first draft and show the world what you're made of. However, there's a certain art to the presentation of a good screenplay; time to make your script look as polished as a Hollywood icon on the red carpet.

Firstly, choose software to present your screenplay in industry-standard formatting. If you're still looking, review lesson ten. We can't stress the importance of screenwriting software enough: it does all the hard work of formatting for you, leaving you more time to marvel at your script's genius. But despite software helping you with screenplay formatting, you should still learn how your script should look.

Let's start with the basics: scene headings should always be written in BLOCK CAPITALS (like shouting at someone online), and specify whether the action is taking place outside or inside. Use the abbreviations "`INT.`" for an interior scene and "`EXT.`" for an exterior one, replete with a period.

The next item in the scene heading specifies the location of the scene as simply as possible, for example "`JOSIE'S LIVING ROOM`". Follow this up with a dash and then a word to denote whether the time is day or night. Remember to add spaces between the interior/exterior note, location, and time of day.

Moving on to the action: it should always be written clearly and concisely. No matter how beautiful your prose, overwriting actions can kill a script, making it a torment to read. Your screenplay should look so clear that your reader's eyes can scan the page easily without tripping over a bulky wedge of words.

So limit your scene descriptions to no more than three lines. If you *must* write more, break your scene description into paragraphs to keep it visually digestible.

Character names should be in block capitals the first time they're introduced, alongside the character's age in parentheses. Multiple character names starting with the same letter tend to cause confusion, so avoid that if at all possible.

Aside from when you mention them in character headings, that's the only time you need to format their name in this way. You don't need to be screaming their name or age across your script for no good reason.

Character headings, however, do need to be in block capitals and presented in the center of the page with their dialogue following suit underneath it.

If a character is speaking in a voiceover, add "`V.O.`" next to the name. If your character is actively engaging in the scene but talking *off*-screen, add "`O.C.`" to indicate off-camera or "`O.S.`" for off-screen.

We strongly advise you to avoid using parentheticals in your script unless there's no other way to presume how a line should be read. If you can't avoid adding a descriptor about how the dialogue should be spoken, present it in parentheses, lowercase, and beneath the character heading.

If you have a *sound* that's crucial to the story, it's common practice to present its description in block capitals too.

Now let's change it up and discuss transitions. All scene transitions should also be presented in block capitals, but at the far right of the page, ending with a colon. Scripts generally begin with "FADE IN:" and end with "FADE OUT:".

"SMASH CUT:" is industry standard for when you want to jolt the audience's attention with a bold contrast from the previous scene. "FADE TO WHITE:" is conventionally used when transitioning into a flashback, and "FADE TO BLACK:" for emphasizing a passage of time between scenes. Your writer's instinct will guide you on how to use these transitions, but if in doubt, dip into a screenplay you respect for inspiration.

Avoid being discarded immediately by decision makers reading your script by following these rules to a tee. Think of your script as the ultimate sales pitch for your talent. So present it as perfectly as possible to ensure that someone, somewhere will be desperate to snap it up.

Homework

We know our screenwriting course is the bomb, but it's extremely important to read as many top-notch screenplays as you can get your hands on, too.

Wax on, wax off: Learn discipline from the masters

Read some professional scripts online – it's the best way to absorb proper screenplay presentation.

Next step

Go through your script and ensure all the rules mentioned above have been applied; be thorough!

Resources

Film Daily's Craft section (https://filmdaily.co/craft/) features weekly articles with free smash-hit scripts you can download. Make sure you bookmark our site. (https://filmdaily.co/)

Learn from the greats – download these free scripts

Classic drama screenplays

https://filmdaily.co/craft/download-best-drama-screenplays-for-free/

2018's Oscar-nominated screenplays

https://filmdaily.co/obsessions/read-2018-oscar-nominated-screenplays-for-free/

Action screenplays

https://filmdaily.co/obsessions/gripping-screenplays-read-for-free/

Horror screenplays

https://filmdaily.co/obsessions/read-the-scariest-screenplays-for-free/

Free scripts to download – from us to you

Eternal Sunshine of the Spotless Mind
https://stephenfollows.com/resource-docs/scripts/eternal_sunshine_of_the_spotless_mind.pdf

Good Will Hunting
https://www.scriptreaderpro.com/wp-content/uploads/2015/05/Good-Will-Hunting.pdf

Moonlight
http://www.dailyscript.com/scripts/MOONLIGHT.pdf

Lost in Translation
http://www.dailyscript.com/scripts/lost_in_translation.pdf

Straight Outta Compton
http://www.universalpicturesawards.com/site-content/uploads/2015/08/Straight-Outta-Compton-Screenplay.pdf

The Big Sick
http://www.amazonstudiosguilds.com/wp-content/uploads/2017/12/BIG-SICK_final-script_for-academy.pdf

Get Out
http://www.universalpicturesawards.com/site-content/uploads/2017/09/GET-OUT.pdf

The Bourne Ultimatum
https://www.scriptreaderpro.com/wp-content/uploads/2018/05/Bourne-Ultimatum-The-ilovepdf-compressed.pdf

The Dark Knight
http://www.joblo.com/scripts/The_Dark_Knight.pdf

Die Hard
http://www.screenplaydb.com/film/scripts/die_hard_screenplay.pdf

Oceans 11
http://www.dailyscript.com/scripts/oceans_11.pdf

The Matrix
http://www.dailyscript.com/scripts/the_matrix.pdf

Alien
https://www.avpgalaxy.net/files/scripts/alien-1978-10-04.pdf

Dawn of the Dead
http://www.horrorlair.com/movies/scripts/dawnofthedead_2004.pdf

Final Destination
http://www.horrorlair.com/movies/scripts/dawnofthedead_2004.pdf

It Follows
http://la-screenwriter.com/wp-content/uploads/2016/03/IT-FOLLOWS-2015-by-David-Robert-Mitchell.pdf

The Omen
http://www.dailyscript.com/scripts/Omen.pdf

Scream
https://www.scriptreaderpro.com/wp-content/uploads/2017/10/Scream-min.pdf

Whiplash
http://www.sonyclassics.com/awards-information/whiplash_screenplay.pdf

Hannah and Her Sisters
https://www.scriptreaderpro.com/wp-content/uploads/2017/10/Hannah-and-Her-Sisters.pdf

No Country for Old Men
https://www.raindance.org/download/no-country-old-men/

The Usual Suspects
http://www.screenwrite.in/Screenplays/Usual%2520Suspects,%2520The.pdf

Nightcrawler
http://www.cinemanews.gr/v5/oscars2015/scripts/250889715.pdf

Lady Bird
http://www.la-screenwriter.com/wp-content/uploads/2017/12/LADY-BIRD-clean-shooting-script.pdf

Sex, Lies, and Videotape
http://www.dailyscript.com/scripts/sex_lies_and_video_tapes.html

27.
The cutting room:
Handling rewrites

By now your script is correctly formatted, but that doesn't mean it's finished. Next you'll need to rewrite your script.

The first thing to know is that rewriting is still just writing. That might sound obvious, but a lot of people confuse rewriting with editing. Editing includes changing some directions or moving dialogue to make things flow better. Editing is what you do *after* rewrites, not during. Proofreading is editing, but rewriting isn't.

Rewriting involves moving entire scenes around and applying ruthless cuts to your script in the name of improvement.

Being able to cut your own work is part of being a great writer. It means hitting delete on what could be the most powerful, beautiful dialogue you've ever written, because you can see it fails to serve your story.

If something doesn't move your story forward, it has no place in your script.

Read your script again and don't fuss over any glaring typos you might find. Save those little horrors for later. Now that you have some distance from your script, ask yourself: Does the story convey what you intended?

Be honest with yourself and as cutthroat with the truth as you are with your script. If you find your story isn't quite hitting the mark, it's time to pull out the script scalpel to make some adjustments.

Figure out which scenes you need to alter or remove altogether from your beat sheet. As hard as it may be, usually removing them as a whole is probably the best thing to do. Take a moment to pour one out for your fallen script buddies and have a cry if you need to; just know this is all worth it.

Look at your characters. Are they moving this yarn forward? Are they integral to the piece? No matter how attached you may be, if they're not pulling their weight ya gotta kill your darlings.

Next, consider your protagonist, whether she's active or passive: the one making all the big decisions that drive the plot, or being overshadowed by the supporting cast.

Analyze whether everything is tied to the protagonist's want or need, and whether there's conflict in every scene. If not, it's time to slice and dice your beats. There must be conflict of some type in every scene. Without it there's no drama, and without drama there's no story.

Make sure you're writing in the *present tense* throughout your script. Screenplays need to be read as though the story is literally occuring as you read each sentence. All of your subplots should have a beginning, middle, and end; and all your characters ought to sound distinct – not just variations of your voice.

Once you've combed through the script, tightened the structure, and tidily dispatched all the useless scenes, dialogue, and characters, you can start *editing*.

Embrace the fact that, as a writer, you're naturally prone to overwrite. We all do – it's what makes editing so crucial. Everything probably requires trimming: scene direction *and* dialogue.

If any of it works *without* certain words, get rid of them. Toss 'em in the trash! Feed 'em to the dog! Dump them in a shallow grave! Just keep them out of your script.

If your scene direction consists of long clumps of prose all unavoidably essential, at least split it into paragraphs; no scene direction should be more than three lines.

Ditching all that extra weight dragging your script down will feel liberating, but even after all those cuts, you're not out of the woods yet. You should repeat the rewriting process *at least twice* to ensure your script is the best it possibly can be.

There's no room for sloppiness or errors here. You've poured your blood, sweat, and tears into this little beauty. You want to ensure the end result is just as masterful as you envisioned when the idea occurred to you.

Be vicious, be merciless, and be smart with that screenwriting scalpel. Making those essential cuts can make for a killer script – one you'll be excited and proud to share with the world.

But before you can even consider doing that, you'll need to give your screenplay some solid proofreading. In our next lesson, we'll explain exactly how.

Homework

Time to play "Operation" on your script! (Except this is more like making a *Robocop* – you add back in better things and don't just leave the patient organless.)

Scene surgery

Even if you think it's working well, just move some of your scenes around on your beat sheet and see what the story would be like if it played out in a different order – you never know what can happen. Real writing is being able to cut, so get cutting, too.

Looking at your script objectively will drastically improve your story. Don't let yourself off the hook: if anything doesn't work, remove it.

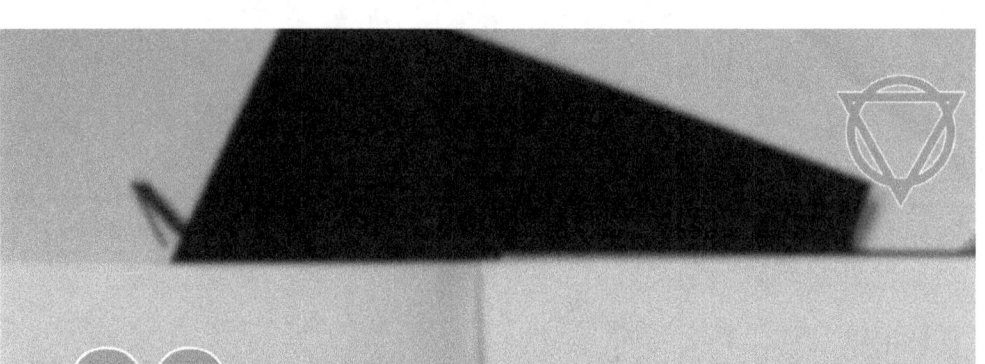

28.
Beg, steal, or borrow a proofreader.

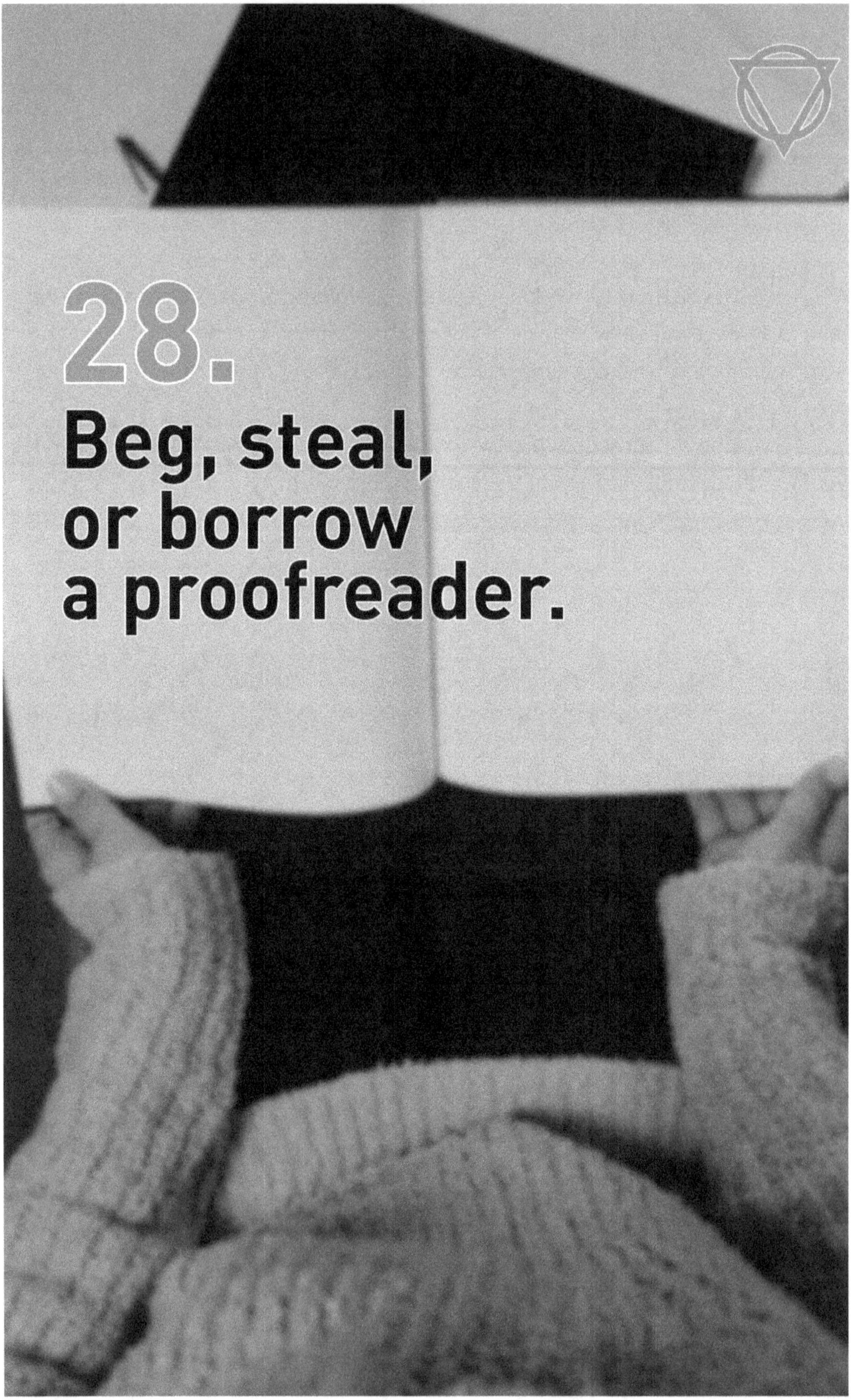

Your screenplay is flowing smoothly, full of punchy dialogue and spunky characters. The masterpiece you've been sweating over is finally complete, and you can't wait to share it with the world.

Tremendous as your writing may be, there's still a chance you missed some glaring typos – even after the third, fifth, or hundredth time you've read through it. The painful reality of proofreading is that you can be blind to your own mistakes.

Because it's your own writing, you know what you're trying to say better than anyone else, so everything you write makes perfect sense in your head – you could fail to see errors right in front of you.

Here's a starter tip for proofing: read your script aloud. Certain mistakes can only be heard rather than read; the human brain has an autocorrect function. Studies even show the brain can piece together a word with only its first and last letters – which can make us even more blind to our own typos.

Reading your work out loud is a great first proofreading step, but what you really need are fresh eyes on that bad boy. In fact, it's *imperative* you find a proofreader to locate all those gnarly blunders you may not have noticed.

If you happen to have a secret stash of cash buried under a squeaky floorboard, you could use it to pay for a professional proofreader. There are proofreading services online, and though they're arguably worth the expense, not everyone can afford them.

The alternative is to find someone you trust to proof for you instead. Make sure they're competent with language and have the grammar skills necessary to see your script's errors.

Another great option is to trade work with another aspiring writer like yourself, so you can analyze and proofread each others' work, a skillshare enterprise that can be a win for everyone involved. Plus, you might even make a new writing friend who isn't your cat.

Proofreading is key, as obvious errors in your script could prevent a reader from wanting to engage any further with it. It's apparent if your screenplay hasn't been proofread, and that comes across as lazy.

Since you're not lazy – you've clearly poured your heart, soul, blood, sweat, and tears into this script – it deserves better than to be riddled with little mistakes that give the wrong impression.

Take the time and the effort to proofread. Your script deserves to be perfect, and the people reading it deserve to enjoy the genius of your story without a single typo to distract them.

Homework

We're nearly at the end of our screenwriting course, so get your masterpiece presentation-ready. If you want your screenplay proofed to the utmost standard and you have a fair bit of cash floating around, check out these sites:

```
https://www.scriptreaderpro.com/proofreading-and-formatting-
service/

https://screenplayreaders.com/product/script-formatting-service/

https://superscreenplays.com/get-started/
```

On a budget? Check this site out.
```
https://www.proofmyspec.com/
```

Next step

Get your script proofread! *Anyone* is better than no one.

29.
Pride comes before a fall:
Every writer needs readers.

A ll any of us can do is make our work the best it can be. We create something then mold it according to our vision; as such, most writing often goes through a process of improvement.

Remember you're writing your script for an audience. That means getting feedback from as many people as possible is the best thing you can do for your script once you've signed off on it.

Be careful to choose the correct people to entrust this fragile bambino of a script to. It might be easier on your ego to give it to folk who will heap nothing but unconstructive praise upon it, but that won't allow this baby to grow.

Instead, you need people who will give you their honest opinion on whether the drama is gripping, the jokes are funny, or the horror is scary. You want readers who'll let you know if a line is a little clichéd, tell you if that bawdy dialogue sounded right coming from a nun, and point out plot holes.

A useful exercise for this is a table read. If you happen to know any aspiring actors with a Sunday night free who don't mind being paid in lasagne, invite them over to read your script. If actors aren't an option – or the lasagne plan doesn't tickle their fancy – then some like-minded friends or fellow screenwriters will also work.

Make sure not to take an active role in a table read. Your job is to sit back, listen to your movie, and take notes on every issue you hear. That means beginning the table read by having someone *else* play the part of narrator by assigning characters to the participants and reading out the actions of the script.

The most common problem you'll likely encounter is people struggling to speak your dialogue, so make careful notes on any line in your script someone has trouble with. You'll likely find some things sounded far better in your head than they do in reality.

By the end, you'll be tempted to offer earnest apologies for the bits you now realize suck beyond belief, but we urge you to hold your tongue. Instead, ask people in turn:

- What did they specifically like about your screenplay?
- What parts did they think could improve?
- Did anything fail to make sense?
- Was it easy to read, or was it clunky?

At this early stage, there will likely be plenty of issues with your script; hopefully the people you invited to help you with it are bold enough to be brutally honest about that. It's your job as a writer to have the correct response to feedback and the right attitude to failure. Both can be soul-crushing. But without feedback or failure, your script will never improve – and neither will you as a writer.

Critique is also something you must become familiar with if you're hoping to make a name for yourself in the industry. Once your screenplay is in development with a production company, it will receive reams of feedback and could be chopped up and changed time and again.

Your professionalism in handling that feedback will help build your reputation. It's crucial to train yourself to be easy to work with and embrace feedback as a gift – not an insult. The industry takes no prisoners, and getting used to absolutely savage notes will prepare you for that. Take on board your collaborators' ideas (and maybe even those of laypersons), and both you and your work will benefit.

Ask readers for the most brutal, honest takes they can give. Insist they stop being polite and start getting *real*. So long as they balance the harsher sides of their criticism by highlighting the strengths of your script, you'll be able to take their constructive criticism.

If you choose to hear only the positives about your screenplay, it might remain a trash fire forever – albeit with a couple moments of potential genius. There's no point in having others read your script if all you seek is ego stroking (however nice a good stroking can be).

Instead, prepare yourself for the worst. Go in with the idea that your script is one level beneath the poop emoji in terms of brilliance, so that any feedback you receive won't feel like a slap in the face.

Making art is hard work, and if it were easy, everyone would be doing it! But you're not everyone. You're a warrior of words. Warriors face defeat and still live to slay another day. You will face defeat and still slay that script.

Thank people for their feedback, even at its most savage. They'll feel more comfortable about giving you more suggestions, and you'll be all the better for it.

After a reading, don't jump on your editing software right away. Give your script some space; let it breathe for a few days while you allow all the feedback to sink in.

Wait until your mind is feeling fresh enough to tackle those final rewrites so you can masterfully add those finishing touches. Then your script will finally be ready to share with the world.

In our next lesson, we'll prep you on where to take your script to be seen, celebrated, and possibly even shopped once your final draft's in hand.

Homework

Listening to your script come alive is how you find those clunky bits of dialogue: what makes sense, continuity errors, and more.

The moment of truth

If you don't already have people with whom you can organize a table read, find groups online. There are hundreds of communities out there that live for this stuff, and you may be surprised at the help you find.

Tit for tat

If you feel awkward meeting a group of strangers in an online group, try to get someone to give you notes on your script. If this person's also a writer, offer to exchange notes. Judging another's script can be one of the best ways to learn.

Find your Coen Brother

Look for online groups devoted to finding like-minded people in film. You never know – you may just find your writing partner out there!

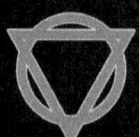

30.
Make the fat lady sing:
Give birth to your script baby.

This is it – the grand climax of your very own hero's journey as an up-and-coming screenwriter. Congratulations! Take a moment to drink in the sense of pride at your screenplay's final draft and give yourself a well deserved pat on the back.

Before we get started with the lesson, we're going to let you in on a little secret: the industry is not as closed off to newcomers as it may appear. If you're truly committed and passionate about the art of screenwriting, you should work hard at honing your craft and put yourself forward for opportunities.

Don't let rejection be off-putting. Instead, learn from missteps, continue to practice screenwriting, improve a little more, and try again. As long as you go about getting your talent noticed in the appropriate manner, you'll eventually succeed in your dream. The cream always rises to the top.

Now, what to do with that slammin' script of yours?

One avenue is to enter it into film festivals. There are hundreds, maybe thousands, all over the world, even festivals geared towards specific genres, or spotlighting work made by or about women, people of color, the LGBTQI community, and more.

Film festivals can give your film prestige and the chance to be screened and seen by people. They also provide invaluable networking opportunities with fellow filmmakers as well as industry professionals seeking out new talent.

Another option is to enter your script into any and every competition you can find. There are plenty of social media screenwriting groups and online resources where you can find listings and information about upcoming contests worth submitting to.

Screenwriting competitions are the best way to ensure your script will be read by professionals. The readers are specifically looking for diamonds in the rough: writers who might not be quite at professional level yet, but possess an original voice, fresh ideas, and other glimmering facets of talent.

The online services FilmFreeway and Withoutabox both contain thousands of film festivals and competitions for all genres and film lengths. Winning a screenwriting competition is something that could potentially attract an agent, making it more likely your work will be read by your favorite production companies.

One thing we advise you *not* to do is email your script to big production companies. Unless they specify they're currently accepting unsolicited screenplay submissions, it's a waste of your time and theirs. In fact, it's likely nobody will even open your email, never mind read your script.

The reality is they probably don't have the time to read your unwelcome script, and the very fact you've approached them in this way will scream "amateur". You can do better.

The screenwriting game is a marathon, not a sprint. It requires hard work and patience, rather than simply hoping for fast fame and lucky breaks.

The last thing to try is to get your script made into an actual film with like-minded aspiring filmmakers. Try to find someone who wants to direct a short film, but lacks a script. This is the person with whom you can raise that fragile bambino of a script! Together you can build a cast and crew, and bring that dynamite script of yours to life on the screen.

You might be tempted to saddle up beside the director and help her do her job – but *don't*. Assist the director and consult with her on the material, but don't micromanage her – or the rest of your team, for that matter. We'll delve into how you should be managing your creative team during our next and final lesson.

Homework

You've done it! We're so proud. It's time to start throwing your script around like you're handing out flyers.

Get hunting

Get online and look for every damn screenwriting competition you can possibly find. Hit up networking events, and bring a copy or two of your script along in case anyone wants to make a short film, but needs a script.

Get on FilmFreeway and Withoutabox, and start hunting for anything and everything – you'll find most of the opportunities are for short films.

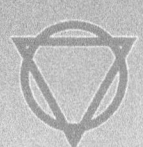

31.
Manage – don't micromanage – your creative team.

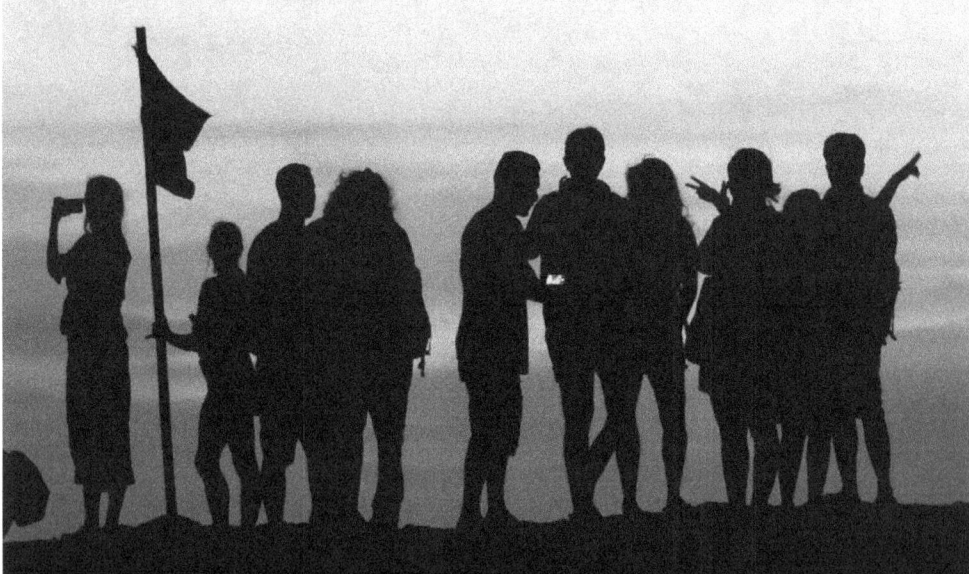

We've already enlightened you about why it's a bad idea for your script to contain director notes like camera angles or soundtrack suggestions. But let us stress the point once more: you're a writer – *not* a director. Write it on the back of your hand if you need to: directors direct, and writers write. It sounds simple, but many aspiring screenwriters still make the mistake of directing actors in their script.

Actors bring their own craft and magic to a film, so allow them some space to experiment and inject their own life into your characters. You might be tempted to write parentheticals or underline certain words for emphasis, but *don't*. Good dialogue shouldn't need specifying.

It can also be effective to write the occasional transition in a script, but do it too often and you'll be stepping on the toes of the editor. Just like actors and directors, editors have a crucial role to play, so let them work their magic without your interference.

After development, production issues often arise that require changes in your script. For instance, the team may lose access to a pivotal set location at the last minute, requiring a script alteration to accommodate the new setting.

Such issues are so common that directors and producers spend much of their careers troubleshooting problems. It could even be argued that good film production is primarily problem-solving.

We know you love your little bambino of a script. You want to see it handled with care and respect, and fostered exactly how you see fit. It can be difficult to let go and trust it in the hands of someone else – but it has to be done. The sooner you accept the script must change in order to be filmed, the easier you will find the process. Being precious about every last detail will get you nowhere.

Learn to embrace change rather than fight it, otherwise your film may never get made. Daily problems occur in production, and sometimes even the most minor issue can alter how your script is being told. That's just the way it is.

Recall George Lucas's highly anticipated and absurdly disappointing *Star Wars* prequels of the early 2000s. They're memorable for all the wrong reasons, and not just due to bad dialogue about sand and a clumsy Gungan military commander called Jar Jar. These films becoming the cinematic equivalent of the Pac-Man death noise is reportedly due to Lucas's micromanagement.

Lucas was apparently determined to do everything himself – he wrote, directed, and produced the *Star Wars* prequels. Via his micromanagement, the whole enterprise understandably turned into a nightmare.

Because Lucas seemed so intent on proving he could do everything, the scripts suffered. The conflict was unclear; the characters' motivations were absent or unrelatable; the pace slowed to a snail's pace with scene after scene of turgid exposition.

Great acting talents like Natalie Portman and Samuel L. Jackson went to waste due to the abominable dialogue. The characters were flat – have we mentioned Jar Jar? Lucas is still convinced the much-maligned character was a success. That's *exactly* what happens when you refuse to listen to critique.

Lucas even allegedly micromanaged hair and makeup to ensure Ewan McGregor's jedi bouffant was exactly how he wanted it! If that doesn't raise alarm bells, we don't know what does.

Lucas's inability to relinquish enough control may have ruined those films. The glaring missteps made with the *Star Wars* prequels are proof that even an experienced movie mogul can fail spectacularly by not trusting others to assist in realizing his vision.

In contrast, *The Empire Strikes Back* was one of the best films of the *Star Wars* franchise, likely because Lucas merely came up with the story idea and world building – his best skills – and stepped back to let a creative team fulfill the rest of the vision. Others wrote the screenplay and directed it.

If you want your script baby to grow, you have to let it go. Trust that your creative team is just as invested in making the best movie possible as you were when writing it. The story doesn't belong solely to you anymore, but to the whole team.

We want *you* to grow, so we have to let you go too. We're wiping a salty tear from our eyes and bidding our farewell, as the end of our screenwriting crash course has finally arrived. Hopefully you've gained vital insight into the craft of screenwriting and feel ready to take the industry by storm. Go get 'em, tiger!

Good luck – and we'll see you at the Oscars.

Homework

Print off your final script if you haven't already. Kick back, grab a brewski or a cuppa tea, and read through all your hard work. Bask in your excellence!

We're getting teary with how proud we are. Well done – go take on the world!

Epilogue

And so your journey as a FilmCraft student is over – and your new journey is about to begin.

You now have the highly sought-after knowledge to craft captivating characters so rich they'll stick in your audience's mind forever. You can structure story so tightly you'll have Tarantino scratching his ugly chin at how you've held his attention without talking about Big Macs. Your scenes are so slick and seamless readers won't know what hit them. All they'll know for sure is they loved it!

We're sorry, kids – school is not out for the summer. As they say in that song, you've "only just begun". Feel free to take the night off, though, and celebrate your finished masterwork.

What now?

Bear with us while we drill down further on some of the points we covered in the past chapters. We want you to succeed, so stay with us while we set you on the best path towards your future.

Organize a table read

Reading your script around a table is loved and hated by filmmakers in equal measures. Some swear by it, while others loathe it. We're in the former category. It's great to hear real humans reading your script – an extremely effective way to see if your dialogue actually works when spoken aloud.

Let your script sit with you for a short time, then organize your table read. First thing's first: get a big net on a stick and bag some actors! Maybe don't try Paltrow or Gosling, they're kinda busy. Instead, contact some local theatre groups or acting schools and see if they'd be interested in a readthrough of a developing script. You'd be surprised at how keen actors can be to try out new work. Their enthusiasm is infectious and you'll end up having a great time.

Live in the back of beyond, with not a single am-dram club in sight? Don't despair – scrape the barrel, treat your friends and family to Domino's, and get them to play the role of actor for the night. Don't be upset by their inexperience; remember, they're doing *you* the favor.

When hosting the table read, consider filming or recording it (if the actors give their consent) so you can keep learning from the experience. Crack open the San Pellegrino and lay out the goji berries. Healthy snacks and drinks will keep everyone's energy levels on fleek so you can get the most out of your actors. During the readthrough, pay close attention to the actors' mood when reading the dialogue. If your actors are having a ton of fun, usually it means they understand their characters' goals and motivations, and are digging the writing. If they look pained or confused, carve time in your schedule for conducting some solid rewrites. You'll know immediately which dialogue pops and locks – and which just flops.

Encourage feedback from your actors – you need all the opinions you can get. Learn to embrace others' thoughts with open arms, instead of going red in the face in frustration whenever someone doesn't understand something in your script. The truth is, everyone knows a good story when they see one. If the actors think it needs work, they're probably right. You just gotta suck it up and find where it isn't working. Take a breather from your script for a day or two and allow the notes to digest, then get cracking with another rewrite.

Protect your work

While we believe an idea is only as good as its execution, screenwriters are a suspicious lot who worry that someone is going to steal their concept. Sleep easier by registering your script with the Writers Guild of America. For a small fee, you can officially register that idea as your own, proving when you initially came up with the idea.

Register your screenplay (`https://www.wgawregistry.org/registration.asp`) for only $20 (members $10) at the WGA.

If your concept is nothing more than a concept at this stage, the WGA also accepts treatments, essentially engaging summaries of a story idea. Treatments are often requested by producers, as they rarely have time to read through a whole feature script. Regardless of its length, it's good practice to treatment your story before writing it.

Get that script outta here!

You may have noticed we highly recommend getting as much feedback as humanly possible. In the last few lessons, we encouraged you to join social media and whatever Meetup groups you could find to network like hell, and gather a large source of like-minded people likely to provide valuable feedback on your script.

If you feel a need for professional script feedback, there are many services online that can do that for you. We've made it easy for you and found our top three contenders for you to consider:

Our favorite is Industrial Scripts (`https://screenplayscripts.com/`). They provide feedback for all lengths of script, from short film to TV pilot to feature screenplay. A short film script report from them costs approximately **$90** – unbeatable feedback from industry professionals you'd struggle to find anywhere else.

Another contender worth checking out is Script Pipeline (`http://scriptpipeline.com/shop/studio-style-coverage`). Their services include incomplete script reads, a rarity. They also provide feedback on TV series bibles and treatments. This will set you back about **$225**.

Last but not least, if you have a thick skin and want brutally honest feedback just like you'd receive in the industry, then Story Sense (`http://www.storysense.com/serv-coverage.htm`) is for you. Their story analyst Michael Ray Brown has over twenty-five years' experience in this game and will give you the cold hard facts about your work: not for the fainthearted, but seriously useful. Approximately **$225**.

The Black List
https://blcklst.com/

The Black List is an increasingly popular website run and used by the hottest professionals in Hollywood. For a fee of approximately $75 dollars, you can submit your script to the list. Professionals looking for the next great story will read scripts on the list and provide a rating. Your script will move up the list the more high ratings you get – and vice versa. This can provide you with a realistic view of where your script currently stands amid fierce competition. Thankfully in this day and age, we don't have to fly out to LA to shop our script – get it on The Black List and let the internet do the work for you.

Screenwriting prizes

Starting a career as a writer is fiendishly difficult, and a boost such as winning a screenwriting competition can make or break it. Once again we've made it easy for you and compiled a list of competitions that can help give you the career boost you need.

Film Daily Screenwriting Contest
https://filmdaily.co/screenwriting-contest-2018/

That's right – we've got your back once again! We have script competitions for every genre and script length you could ever think of. The winner of each contest wins a Skype one-to-one with an industry professional to help with where to go next, along with some professional screenwriting software!

The Academy Nicholls Fellowship
http://www.oscars.org/nicholl

There are five winners receiving bursaries up to $35,000 each, along with a year-long development placement in which you're guided in improving your work by the best of the best. This really is the mother of all fellowships, supported as it is by a small-time awards academy – some might know it as the Oscars.

Austin Film Festival
https://austinfilmfestival.com/submit/screenplay-and-teleplay-submissions-2/

With a special category for short films and teleplays, this festival is affordable and recognized worldwide as one the most established screenplay competitions. They even provide script coverage services if you feel your script is not as good as it could be. Winners receive meetings with managers and agents, all there to try and establish a relationship and start your career.

These are just some of the many competitions you can enter to get ahead – but beware of screenwriting contest scams. Do your research before entering. God bless the internet!

Screenwriting events and meetups

Remember networking is key to this game, so get out there! The Black List hosts monthly screenwriting meetups in cities all over the US, and Montreal and London as well. Though there are many film festivals, there are just as many screenwriting festivals, usually free or cheap to attend. Make friends, take workshops with rad writers, and secure industry connections, all in one weekend!

Screenwriter groups are becoming more popular as they provide a gateway for folks who have no industry connections to gain them. Search on the web for writer groups near you and you'll be surprised at how many are out there. Pick the one that's right for you to hone your craft in. You'll be providing feedback for other people's screenplays too, which will train your critical eye.

Don't want to wait? Find collaborators and become an executive producer. If you want to learn how to do that, you'll just have to read our next book all about producing. Sign up for our newsletter and we'll send you a free excerpt.

Happy writing!
– The FilmCraft Team

Bibliography

Day 1

A Trip to the Moon, 1902 [film]. Directed by George Melies. France: Star Films

The Great Train Robbery, 1903 [film]. Directed by Edwin S. Porter. USA. Edison Manufacturing Company

Day 2

Employees leaving the Lumiere Factory, 1895 [film]. Directed by Louis Lumiere. France: Lumiere

A Trip to the Moon, 1902 [film]. Directed by George Melies. France: Star Films

The Great Dictator, 1940 [film]. Directed by Charlie Chaplin. USA: Charles Chaplin Productions

Day 3

The Killing, 1956 [film]. Directed by Stanley Kubrick. USA: Harris-Kubrick Productions

Electronic Labyrinth THX 1138 4EB 1967 [film]. Directed by George Lucas. USA: University of Southern California

Boy and Bicycle 1965 [film]. Directed by Ridley Scott. UK: British Film Institute (BFI)

The Big Shave 1967 [film]. Directed by Martin Scorcese. USA:

Gasman 1997 [film]. Directed by Lynne Ramsey. UK: BBC, Holy Cow Films, Scottish Arts Council

Whiplash 2013 [film]. Directed by Damien Chazelle. USA

The Simpsons 1989 [TV]. Creators: James L. Brooks, Matt Groening, Sam Simon. USA: 20th Century Fox

The Tracey Ullman Show 1987 [TV] Directed by Ted Bessel. USA: 20th Century Fox

Broad City 2010 [TV] Directed by Rob Michael Hugel. USA

The Misadventures of Awkward Black Girl 2011 [TV] Created by Issa Rae. USA: Issa Rae Productions

Insecure 2016 [TV] Directed by Melina Matsoukas. USA: 3 Arts Entertainment

Day 4

Inside Out 2015 [film] Directed by Pete Docter, Ronnie Del Carmen. USA: Pixar Animation Studios, Walt Disney Pictures

Game of Thrones 2011 [TV] Directed by David Nutter. USA, UK: HBO

The Writer's Journey [book] Third Edition. Written by Vogler, C. 1998. USA: Michael Wiese Productions

Titanic 1997 [film] Directed by James Cameron. USA: 20th Century Fox

Day 5

In Cold Blood 1966 [book] Capote, T. USA: Random House

Day 6

Phantom Thread 2017 [film] Directed by Paul Thomas Anderson. USA, UK: Focus Features

The Writer's Workbook 1984 [book] Written by Field, S. USA: Bantam Dell

Day 7

Phone Booth 2002 [film] Directed by Joel Schumacher. USA: Fox 2000 Pictures

Reservoir Dogs 1992 [film] Directed by Quentin Tarantino. USA: Live Entertainment

Day 9

It's Always Sunny in Philadelphia 2005 [TV] Directed by Matt Shakman. USA: Bluebush Productions

Silicon Valley 2014 [TV] Directed by Mike Judge. USA: 3 Arts Entertainment

The Good Place 2016 [TV] Directed by Dean Holland. USA: Fremulon

Rick and Morty 2013 [TV] Directed by Pete Michels. USA: Harmonious Claptrap

Riverdale 2016 [TV] Directed by Lee Toland Krieger. USA: Berlanti Productions

Day 12

Colossal 2016 [film] Directed by Nacho Vigalondo. Canada, USA, Spain, South Korea: Toy Fight Productions

Glow 2017 [TV] Directed by Sian Heder. USA: Netflix

Rick and Morty 2013 [TV] Directed by Pete Michels. USA: Harmonious Claptrap

Community 2009 [TV] Directed by Tristram Shapeero. USA: Krasnoff Foster Productions

Day 13

The Walking Dead 2010 [TV] Directed by Greg Nicotero. USA: American Movie Classics (AMC)

Angela (2013, Oct 3) Structuring Your Script With the Dan Harmon Story Circle, `http://www.la-screenwriter.com/2013/10/03/structuring-your-script-with-the-dan-harmon-story-circle/`

Day 14

Save The Cat 2005 [book] Written by Snyder, B. Michegan, USA: Michael Wiese Productions

Day 15

Suicide Squad 2016 [film] Directed by David Ayer. USA: Atlas Entertainment

A Quiet Place 2018 [film] Directed by John Krasinski. USA: Platinum Dunes

Jumanji: Welcome to the Jungle 2017 [film] Directed by Jake Kasdan. USA: Columbia pictures

Lady Bird 2017 [film] Directed by Greta Gerwig. USA: Scott Rudin Productions

Day 17

Black Panther 2018 [film] Directed by Ryan Coogler. USA: Marvel Studios

Darkest Hour 2017 [film] Directed by Joe Wright. UK, USA: Perfect World Pictures

Valerian and the City of a Thousand Planets 2017 [film] France, China, Belgium, Germany, United Arab Emirates, USA: Europacorp

The Shape of Water 2017 [film] Directed by Guillermo del Toro. USA: Bull Productions

Day 18

Story 1998 [book] Written by McKee, R. USA: Regan Books

RuPaul's Drag Race 2009 [TV] Directed by Nick Murray. USA: World of Wonder Productions

Westworld 2016 [TV] Directed by Richard J. Lewis. USA: Bad Robot

Blade Runner 2049 2017 [film] Directed by Denis Villeneuve. USA, UK, Hungry, Canada: Alcon Entertainment

Day 19

Three Billboards Outside Ebbing Missouri 2017 [film] Directed by Martin McDonagh. UK, USA: Blueprint Pictures

Day 20

The Shape of Water 2017 [film] Directed by Guillermo del Toro. USA: Bull Productions

Get Out 2017 [film] Directed by Jordan Peele. Japan, USA: Universal Pictures

Big Little Lies 2017 [film] Directed by Jean-Marc Vallee. USA: Blossom Films

Riverdale 2016 [TV] Directed by Lee Toland Krieger. USA: Berlanti Productions

Black Panther 2018 [film] Directed by Ryan Coogler. USA: Marvel Studios

Day 21

The Room 2003 [film] Directed by Tommy Wiseau. USA: Wiseau-films

Day 22

Westworld 2016 [TV] Directed by Richard J. Lewis. USA: Bad Robot

Day 23

Riverdale 2016 [TV] Directed by Lee Toland Krieger. USA: Berlanti Productions

Westworld 2016 [TV] Directed by Richard J. Lewis. USA: Bad Robot

The Walking Dead 2010 [TV] Directed by Greg Nicotero. USA: American Movie Classics (AMC)

The Americans 2013 [TV] Directed by Chris Long. USA: Amblin Television

Riverdale 2016 [TV] Directed by Lee Toland Krieger. USA: Berlanti Productions

Day 24

La La Land 2016 [film] Directed by Damien Chazelle. USA, Hong Kong: Summit Entertainment

Day 31

Star Wars Episode I: The Phantom Menace 1999 [film] Directed by George Lucas. USA: Lucasfilm

Star Wars Episode V: The Empire Strikes Back 1980 [film] Directed by Irvin Kershner. USA: Lucasfilm

Star Wars Episode VI: Return of the Jedi 1983 [film] Directed by Richard Marquand. USA: Lucasfilm

We learned from these books (and you should too)

Vogler, C 1998, *The Writer's Journey,* Third Edition, Michael Wiese Productions, USA

McKee, R 1998, *Story,* Regan Books, USA

Field, S 2003, *The Definitive Guide to Screenwriting,* Ebury Press, Great Britain

Field, S 1984, *The Writer's Workbook,* Bantam Dell, USA

Snyder, B 2005, *Save The Cat,* Michael Wiese Productions, Michegan, USA

Yorke, J 2013, *Into the Woods,* Penguin Books, Milton Keynes, UK

Websites we love
(and you should too)

The L.A. Screenwriter
http://www.la-screenwriter.com/

The No Film School
https://nofilmschool.com/

Script Magazine
http://www.scriptmag.com/

The Black List
https://blcklst.com/

IMDb
https://www.imdb.com/

Simply Scripts
http://www.simplyscripts.com/

Script Reader Pro
https://www.scriptreaderpro.com/

Raindance
https://www.raindance.org/

Scribendi
https://www.scribendi.com/

Seth Godin
https://www.sethgodin.com/

The Four-Hour Work Week
https://fourhourworkweek.com/

FilmFreeway
https://filmfreeway.com/

Withoutabox
https://www.withoutabox.com/

Netflix
https://www.netflix.com/

Hulu
https://www.hulu.com/

Amazon Video
https://www.amazon.com/USA-Instant-Video/b?ie=UTF8&node=363238011

MUBI
https://mubi.com/

Shudder
https://www.shudder.com/

Vimeo
https://vimeo.com/

YouTube
https://www.youtube.com/

Facebook Watch
https://www.facebook.com/watch

www.ingramcontent.com/pod-product-compliance
Lightning Source LLC
Chambersburg PA
CBHW052316220526
45472CB00001B/143